Quick
Knits
with
Today's
Yarns

Jayne S. Davis

©2005 Jayne S. Davis

Published by

kp books
An Imprint of F+W Publications

700 East State Street • Iola, WI 54990-0001
715-445-2214 • 888-457-2873

Our toll-free number to place an order or obtain a free catalog is
(800) 258-0929.

Library of Congress Catalog Number: 2004097733
ISBN: 0-87349-994-8

Edited by Maria L. Turner
Designed by Donna Mummery

Printed in the United States of America

Dedication

To Jodie Davis Barthlow—
stepdaughter by chance, friend by
choice, partner by destiny.

Acknowledgments

In any undertaking such as this, there are many helping hands.
Special thanks go to the yarn companies and suppliers who stepped up to the plate
to help make this all possible.
Your local yarn shop is a wealth of inspiration and mine are no exception.
Thank you to longtime friend Bebby Weigand at Penelope's Breads and Threads
and Harriet Cohen at Yarns by Justharri, both in Delray Beach, Fla., and the staff
at ImaginKnit in Lake Worth, Fla.
My fondest thanks go to my editor, Maria Turner, who took this book novice by
the hand and led me through the labyrinth.
Thanks to Julie Stephani for getting the ball rolling and all of you at
KP Books, including page designer Donna Mummery, cover designer Marilyn
McGrane and illustrator Melinda Bylow for making everything work.
And thank you John, my husband, for being so supportive and never asking
about dinner or mentioning the dust balls or asking why I was staring at a
blank computer screen. Thank you especially for bringing your two wonderful
daughters, Christie Bright and Jodie Davis Barthlow, into my life.

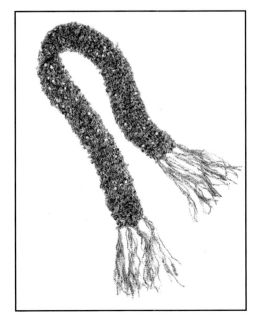

Table of Contents

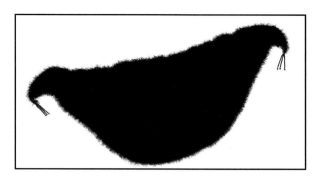

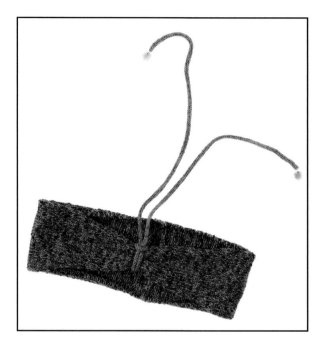

Foreword

Have you taken a gander at the yarn aisle of your favorite crafts store lately?

A smorgasbord of enticing delicacies has upstaged yesterday's bland acrylic yarns. From the exotic to the luxuriant, these luscious skeins cause the creative muse's mouth to water. If you're like me, you're having a tough time resisting the temptation. Except for one little problem: I'm a quilter; I don't knit!

But when Jayne handed me this manuscript, I could see that this quilter needn't be a knitter to turn a few balls of exquisite yarn into a worthwhile project. This book is written with the non-knitter in mind. Using only the simplest of stitches, even I can make a great project, for it is today's yarns that turn the would-be simple into the sublime. Oh, to indulge myself!

Which brings me to something we all know about, but often fight within ourselves. We creative types tend to be interested in many things, specializing in one. Some go from one medium to another, delving chin deep into the craft and becoming proficient before answering the beckoning whispers of another calling. Others become solely smitten and pursue their passion for years. Either way, every creative person I've ever met has something in common: They don't do just one thing. Some quilters make dolls. Some potters paint fabric. Some painters have uniquely personal homes of their creation, while others paint with flowers in their yards. And how many creative friends do you have who garden and cook? Seems to come with the territory more often than not.

The creative muse relishes a novel excursion now and again. In my early years, I saw this as a negative. I thought, "I should stick to what it is I do, not allow myself to be sidetracked by this candy store of a world." Over time, I have discovered that all of this—this big world of wonderful things to do—is part of my quilting, fodder for the hungry wood-burning cook stove that maintains my passion at a good simmer. When I garden, I am playing with color and texture; when I sculpt a rubber duck, stencil a floor cloth for my porch or stitch and glue a creepy Halloween decoration for my front door, the creative process is exactly the same as with anything else. I am carving, painting or sewing an internal vision into real form, an expression from within. Creativity cross-pollinates.

As with any journey, one returns home richer for adding another ingredient to the pantry of images, ideas and experiences that nourish the creative heart. See, everything has to do with everything else!

So, I am setting aside the quilting needle and heading off to the knitting shop, book in hand, ready for a new adventure with the novel feel of knitting needles. The next time you see me, I may be wearing my very own knitted scarf!

Jodie Davis
Jodie and Company, Inc.

Introduction

What ancient craft has found its way to the forefront again? Knitting, of course. With today's gorgeous yarns in a multitude of textures and hues the possibilities are endless.

This book showcases 50 stylish projects made with these wonderful yarns, using just the knit and purl stitches. These two simple stitches are used in endless combinations to make a myriad of easy-to-do patterns. Wraps, jackets, hats, socks, purses and knitted jewelry are included.

For the novice and those of us who could use a brush-up course, a complete primer on basic equipment and basic knitting and finishing techniques are included along with helpful hints.

All of the projects can stand on their own; however, many have added embellishments of beads, buttons, charms, fringes, pompoms and even handmade trims. Such additions give each project an added pizzazz. If that's too over-the-top for you, just leave them off. After all, it's *your* project.

Remember that your local yarn shop is a candy box full of goodies and the staff is there to help. Visit your local craft store for add-ons, and if there is a bead shop nearby, do take a look. The Internet is also a wonderful tool for seeing what is available in the marketplace. Be sure to turn to the Resources section in this book, page 128, for a partial guide. The world really is at our fingertips today.

Time was, women knitted from necessity. Today, we knit for the sheer joy.

Knitting beautiful objects is what this book is all about. Let's start the journey.

Getting Started

We all know what a knitted hat or scarf or bag looks like, but how do we get from a picture to a finished project? This chapter gives you all the answers, from the tools you will need to the yarns to use to the how-to information to guide you. What fun you will have wearing or giving that special knitted treasure!

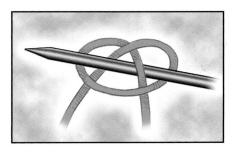

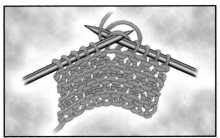

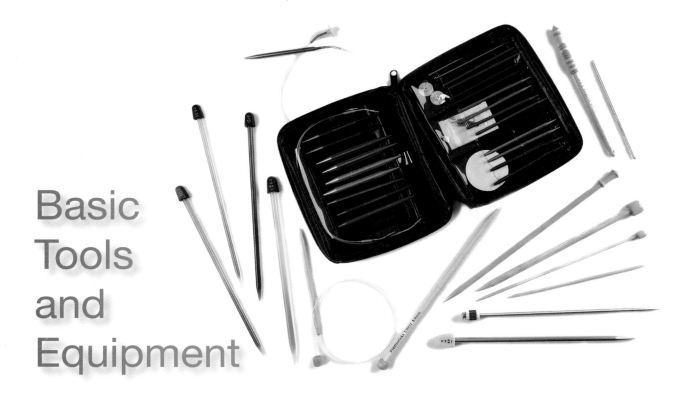

Basic Tools and Equipment

Knitting needles are your primary tool.

Needles come in a wide range of sizes, types and lengths and are made of a variety of materials, including aluminum, plastic, wood and even bamboo.

Basic needles are pointed on one end and come in 10" and 14" lengths and are sold in pairs. Standard United States sizes range from 0 to 15 and come in even larger sizes for bulkier yarns. Many needles are marked with both U.S. sizes and the diameter in millimeters.

Circular needles are used to knit projects in a tube without a seam.

Besides needles, an array of useful knitting accessories is available in the marketplace. It's always fun to have an "I could use that" moment.

Double-pointed needles are sold in sets of four or five and are used to make small, round projects.

Flex needles are straight single-point needles sold in pairs with a firm portion for forming the stitch and a super-flexible nylon shaft that allows much wider work to be held on the needles.

KNITTING NEEDLES CONVERSION

American	Metric (mm)	American	Metric (mm)	American	Metric (mm)
0	2.00	6	4.25	-	7.00
1	2.25	7	4.50	-	7.50
2	2.75	8	5.00	11	8.00
-	3.00	-	5.25	13	9.00
3	3.25	9	5.50	15	10.00
4	3.50	-	5.75	17	13.00
5	3.75	10	6.00	19	15.00
-	4.00	10½	6.50		

You'll always need a pair of **small scissors** and a **measuring tape**.

Crochet hooks are useful to pick up dropped stitches and to add crocheted edgings to projects.

Point protectors do just what their name implies: protect the ends of your needles and keep stitches from slipping off the needles between knitting sessions.

Row counters help you keep track of the number of rows knitted, which is necessary when working patterns. They slip right on your needles. Just turn the dial as you finish each row.

Special long pins with large heads are used to pin pieces together for sewing.

A **stitch gauge** is a handy gadget to measure your knitting gauge. Some also have a **needle gauge** to check the needle size if the markings have worn off the needles.

Stitch markers are rings that are slipped from needle to needle to mark increases, decreases and pattern changes. Coil-like markers can be used to mark a particular position, such as a waistline, and are easily removed.

A **yarn needle** or **large-sized tapestry needle** is used to seam finished pieces together or weave in yarn ends.

TIP

Buy needles as you need them for specific projects. Over time, you'll find you've accumulated quite a collection. Keep needles organized and protected in one of the many needle storage bags available at your local yarn store. Take good care of your needles and you'll find they'll last a lifetime.

All About
the Yarns

Walking into a yarn shop puts me in a state of euphoria—all those textures and colors! These wonderful yarns are made from many different materials. Fibers like wool, angora, cashmere, alpaca and mohair come from a variety of animals. Plant fibers include cotton, linen, rayon, silk and even bamboo. Synthetic fibers are manmade and include nylon, polyester and acrylic, to name just a few. Many yarns are blends of various fibers lending the best characteristics of each to the finished yarn.

The types of yarns on the market today seem endless. There are woven, brushed, eyelash, boucle, knitted, nub, chenille and plied yarns, plus yarns that are made up of various combinations.

Yarn is sold in balls, skeins and hanks. You can work directly from balls and skeins since they are wound to prevent the yarn from tangling as you work. Hanks need to be wound into balls. You do this by untwisting the hank so it looks like a thick circle of yarn. Have someone hold the hank stretched firmly between their hands or place it over the back of a kitchen-style chair. Wind it into balls, being careful not to wind too tightly.

Standard Yarn Weight System

Recently, yarn industry designers, manufacturers and publishers adopted a standardized system to help knitters understand the various yarn weights and needle sizes. These symbols, which appear on the yarn labels, are incorporated into each project in this book to make it easier for you to choose your own yarn variations. Use the chart as a guideline, as it reflects the most commonly used gauges and needle sizes for specific yarn categories.

TIPS

• When doing stockinette stitch with heavily textured yarns, you'll find that most of the detail from the nubs, loops and lashes will be found on the purl side. A better choice would be to use garter stitch or reverse stockinette.

• Buy enough yarn at one time to complete the project. If you're not sure, buy an extra skein, as it's better to be safe than sorry. You'll always find a use for the leftover yarn.

• Make sure that all the balls or skeins of yarn you buy of one color are the same dye lot. The colors may all look the same, but you will notice the difference in dye lots in the finished piece. The dye lot number is always marked on the label.

STANDARD YARN WEIGHT SYSTEM

Yarn Weight Symbol and Category Names	1 SUPER FINE	2 FINE	3 LIGHT	4 MEDIUM	5 BULKY	6 SUPER BULKY
Types of Yarns in a Category	Sock, Fingering, Baby	Sport, Baby	DK, Light, Worsted	Worsted, Afghan, Aran	Chunky, Craft, Rug	Bulky, Roving
Knit Gauge Range in St st to 4"	27 to 32 sts	23 to 26 sts	21 to 24 sts	16 to 20 sts	12 to 15 sts	6 to 11 sts
Recommended Metric Needle Size Range	2.25mm to 3.25mm	3.25mm to 3.75mm	3.75mm to 4.5mm	4.5mm to 5.5mm	5.5mm to 8mm	8mm and larger
Recommended U.S. Needle Size Range	#1 to #3	#3 to #5	#5 to #7	#7 to #9	#9 to #11	#11 and larger

Skill Levels

A set of standard skill level icons also was introduced recently to the industry by the Craft Yarn Council of America. Each project in this book contains a skill level icon to guide you.

BEGINNER Projects for first-time knitters, using basic knit and purl stitches and minimal shaping.

EASY Projects using basic stitches, repetitive stitch patterns, simple color changes, and simple shaping and finishing.

INTERMEDIATE Projects with a variety of stitches, such as basic cables and lace, simple intarsia, double-pointed needles and knitting in the round needle techniques, plus mid-level shaping and finishing.

EXPERIENCED Projects using advance techniques and stitches, such as short rows, fair isle, more intricate intarsia, cables, lace patterns, plus numerous color changes.

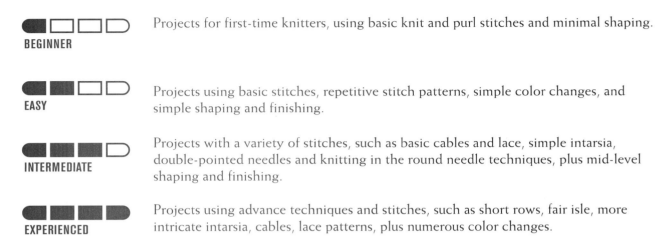

What the Yarn Label Tells You

That piece of paper wrapped around your yarn is packed with useful information. Read the label carefully, as it will give you the following: yarn content; length of yarn in yards and meters; weight in ounces and grams; suggested knitting needle size and the resulting gauge; dye lot number; color name and number; and care instructions.

The care instructions are shown as symbols. This guide will help you decipher what they mean.

Additional symbols appear on labels to designate the various weights or thicknesses of yarns. A number from one to six is assigned, with one the finest weight and six the thickest (see Standard Yarn Weight Systems on page 13).

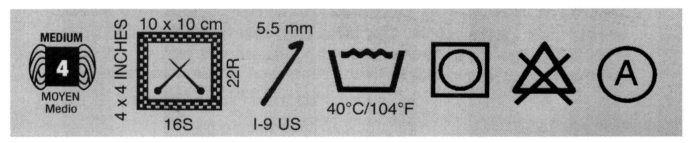

Washing
- Do not wash
- Hand-wash in warm water
- Hand-wash at temperature stated
- Machine wash
- Do not tumble dry
- Tumble drying acceptable
- Dry flat
- No bleach
- Chlorine bleach acceptable

Pressing
- Do not iron
- Cool iron
- Warm iron
- Hot iron

Dry Cleaning Symbols
- Do not dry clean
- (A) Dry cleanable in all solvents
- (F) Dry cleanable with fluorocarbon or petroleum-based solvents only
- (P) Dry cleanable with perchlorethylene, hydrocarbons, or petroleum-based solvent

Basic Techniques

The knitting stitch is nothing but a loop pulled through a loop. This simple loop makes an endless variety of fabrics in countless textures and patterns.

There are two basic styles of knitting—English and continental—and the difference between the two is in how you hold the yarn. In the U.S., the English method is the most common and what will be illustrated within this book.

There are many, many ways to accomplish most of the steps shown and there's not necessarily a best way. To keep things simple, just one method is shown. All work well for the patterns in this book.

AN ASIDE

I'll admit it, I have a hard time discarding things I have put my heart and soul and endless hours into creating. But, the day had come for a terrific sweater I had knitted more than 30 years earlier and had sadly outgrown. My friend Libbie saw me putting it into the "good-bye bag" and said, "Don't throw that away. Give it to me. I love it!" And so, a cherished sweater found a second life.

What's the point of this tale? Yarns are not inexpensive and your time certainly has value. If you're going to spend the time and money to knit something for yourself or to give as a gift, make sure it's worth the effort and will be enjoyed for years to come.

Casting On

The first step in knitting is to put a row of stitches on your needle. This is called casting on and is shown as CO in directions.

The method illustrated is the one I use most often, but there are many other methods. This is called the double cast-on method. It gets its name because you're using two strands from the same skein of yarn.

TIP

Always review the pattern instructions carefully to determine how many stitches to cast-on and how much yarn to measure.

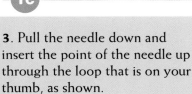

1. Measure off a length of yarn, allowing 1" for each stitch plus a couple of extra inches. Make a slipknot at this point by making a pretzel shape with the yarn and slipping the needle into the pretzel as shown. This is your first stitch.

2. Hold the needle with the slipknot in your right hand and drape the short end of yarn over your left thumb and the yarn from the skein over your index finger. Gently pull the two ends of yarn apart to tighten the loop by spreading your thumb and finger. Be careful not to tighten it too much, since you want the stitch to glide easily over the needle. Rest both strands of yarn in the palm of your hand with the last two fingers holding them down.

3. Pull the needle down and insert the point of the needle up through the loop that is on your thumb, as shown.

4. Move the point of the needle around the strand of yarn on your index finger, as shown.

5. Bring the point of the needle back down through the loop on your thumb.

6. Drop the loop on your thumb.

7. Tighten the stitch by pulling on the short end of the yarn with your thumb. You now have two stitches on your needle.

8. Repeat steps 1 through 7 until you have cast-on the number of stitches needed.

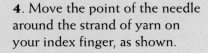

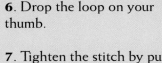

Knit Stitch

Knitting uses just two basic stitches: the knit stitch and the purl stitch. Start with the knit stitch. It is shown as "k" in directions.

TIP

If you're left-handed, don't fret; I am too. Knitting uses both hands and I've never seen any reason to make any adjustments. So, all you left-handers, jump right in.

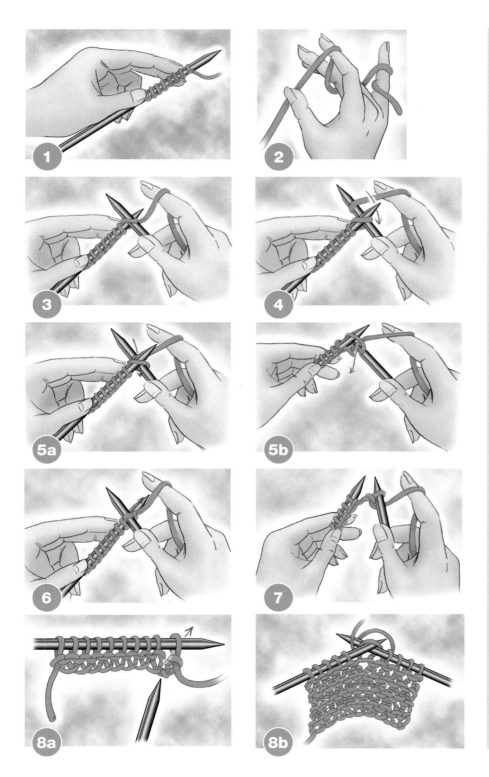

1. Hold the needle with the cast-on stitches in your left hand, with the first stitch near the top, as shown.

2. Hold the empty needle in your right hand and wrap the yarn around your fingers, as shown. This provides the necessary tension.

3. Insert the right needle into the front of the first stitch, slipping it under the left-hand needle.

4. With your right hand, bring the yarn under and over the point of the right needle, as shown.

5. Draw the yarn under the left-hand needle and through the stitch, as shown.

6. Slip the old stitch off the left needle. The first stitch of the row, which is now on the right needle, is complete, as shown.

7. Repeat steps 1 through 4 until all the stitches have been knit off the left needle.

8. When the row is complete, turn the work so the needle with the stitches is in your left hand and begin again, as shown.

Purl Stitch

The purl stitch is the second most basic stitch. It is shown as "p" in directions.

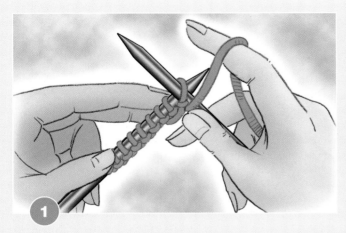

1. Start with the yarn in front of your work and insert the right needle in the stitch from the right, slipping it over the left needle.

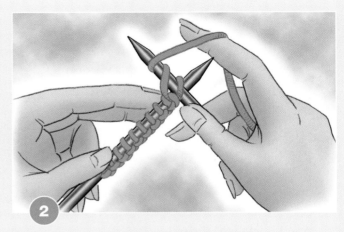

2. Wrap the yarn around the right needle.

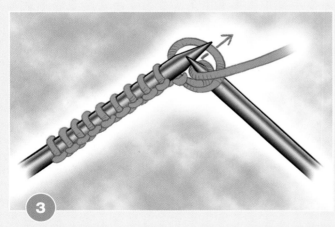

3. Slide the right needle down, bringing the tip from the front to the back through the stitch and the yarn with it.

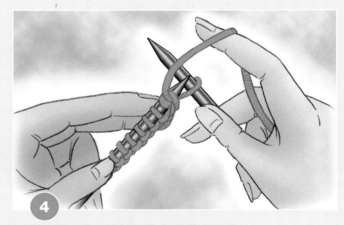

4. Slip the old stitch off the left needle.

5. Repeat steps 1 through 4 until all the stitches have been knitted off the left needle.

6. When the row is complete, turn the work so the needle with the stitches is in your left hand.

Other Stitches

The following stitches are created by using different combinations of the knit and purl stitches.

Garter Stitch is formed when every stitch of every row is worked in knit stitch.

Stockinette Stitch is created by alternating knit and purl rows. The smooth (knit) side is the right side. This stitch is abbreviated as St st.

Reverse Stockinette Stitch is just the opposite of stockinette, as it is made by alternating purl and knit rows. The right side is the bumpy (purl) side. This stitch is abbreviated rev St st.

Seed Stitch (also called moss stitch) is produced by alternating one knit and one purl stitch within a row and then knitting the knit stitches and purling the purl stitches on the return row.

Rib Stitch is the result of alternating knit and purl stitches on one row and then purling the knit stitches and knitting the purl stitches on the return row. The resulting pattern is vertical ridges. The ratio of knit to purl stitches can be even or uneven.

Increasing

This increase is the one most commonly used and is called the plain increase. It can be done anywhere within a row, including the beginning or the end. The abbreviation is "inc."

Increasing in a knit row

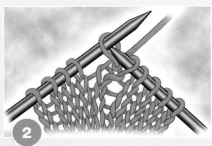

1. Insert the needle into the front of the stitch and knit, but do not slip the worked stitch from the needle.

2. Put the needle into the back of that same stitch and knit another stitch.

Increasing in a purl row

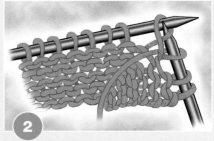

1. Purl the stitch, but do not slip it off the left needle.

2. Insert the right needle into the back of the same stitch, wrapping the yarn as for purling, and draw through another stitch, as shown.

3. Slip the two stitches off the left-hand needle together.

Decreasing

A decrease (dec) takes one stitch away from the total number in the row. This can be done by either knitting two stitches together (k2tog) or purling two stitches together (p2tog), depending on the pattern you are using.

Decreasing in a knit row

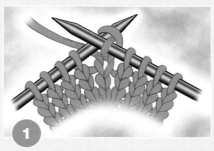

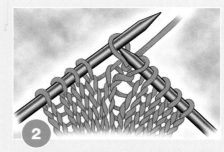

1. Insert the right needle into two stitches at the same time.

2. Continue to make the knit stitch in the usual manner.

Decreasing in a purl row

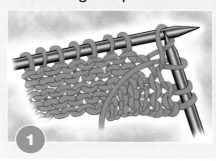

1. Insert the right needles into two stitches at the same time.

2. Purl as if they were one stitch.

Slip the First Stitch

When directions say "slip a stitch" (shown as sl 1), insert the right needle in the stitch to be slipped, as if to purl and simply pass the stitch from the left needle to the right needle without working it.

Adding New Yarn

It's best to attach a new yarn at the beginning of a row.

Sometimes, you will need to attach the yarn in the middle of the row.

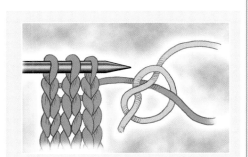

Tie the new yarn in a simple knot over the old yarn, leaving a tail a few inches long, as shown above.

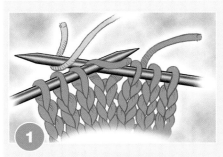

1. Slide the yarn close to the needle and leaving an end of the old yarn, wrap the new yarn around the right needle, as shown, and start knitting.

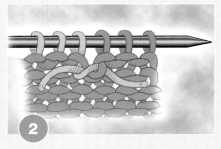

2. Go back, tie a knot and weave the ends in later, as shown above.

HISTORY FLASHBACKS

A piece of plain knitting made thousands of years ago was found in an Egyptian tomb. We don't know anything about that anonymous knitter, but we do know this was a precious object to accompany the soul to the afterlife.

Hundreds of years ago, knitting became a cottage industry in Europe and many women helped support their families by knitting stockings and shawls.

Photo courtesy of Brittany Hooks and Needles.

Binding Off

When you've finished knitting your piece, you're ready to bind off (BO), so it won't unravel. Here is the method used most often.

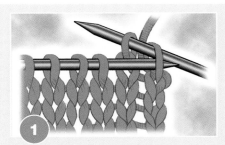

1. Knit the first two stitches of the row, as shown.

2. Using the point of the left needle, lift the first stitch up and over the second stitch and slip it off the needle, as shown. One stitch has been bound off and one remains on the right needle.

3. Knit the next stitch.

4. Lift the first stitch as in step 2.

5. Repeat steps 3 and 4 across the row.

The same method is used for binding off in purl stitch, except the stitches are purled instead of knitted. Always follow your pattern stitch. For instance, if you're binding off a knit2-purl2 ribbing, knit the knit stitches and purl the purl stitches.

TIP

Be sure to bind off loosely. You want the edge to be as elastic as your knitting. If you're having trouble keeping it loose, use a larger size needle.

Finishing Off Last Stitch

One stitch remains on the right needle at the end of the row. Here is how to finish it off:

1. Cut the yarn, leaving a tail several inches long.

2. Pull the tail through the last stitch, as shown at right. If this is a piece that must be joined, leave a sufficient length of yarn to use in seaming.

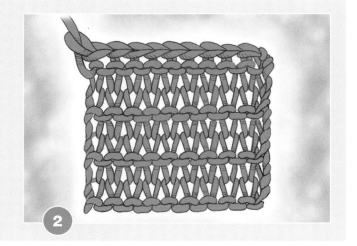

Making an I-Cord

The late Elizabeth Zimmerman was a knitting pioneer who, through her books and classes, taught tens of thousands to "knit outside the box." She's credited with inventing the I-cord, a knitted tube with countless uses. We've used it in this book as purse handles, necklaces and a halter strap.

You'll need two double pointed needles. The needle size depends on the weight of the yarn—the larger the needle, the thicker your I-cord will be.

1. Cast on three stitches and knit every stitch.

2. Slide all the stitches to the other end of the needle.

3. Switch needles in your hands so the needle with the stitches is in your left hand and knit the row again, as shown at right.

4. Continue sliding, switching hands and knitting the row until the cord is the length you want.

5. Bind off all stitches.

Fixing a Mistake

We've all done it—the disastrous dropped stitch. The bad news is that if left alone, it will "run" just like a stocking. The good news is that it's fixable if the stitch has run for just a few rows.

> **TIP**
>
> Constantly look over your knitting as you work, checking it for errors. There's nothing more disconcerting than ripping out hours of work.

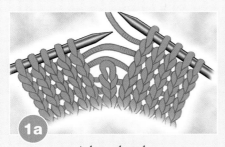

A dropped stitch.

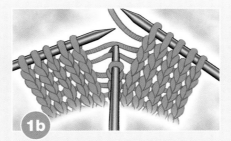

Picking up a knit stitch in stockinette stitch.

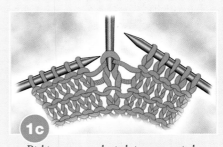

Picking up a purl stitch in garter stitch.

1. Using a crochet hook, catch the loose stitch and draw the horizontal thread of the row above through the loop, as shown.

2. Repeat until you reach the row on which you're working.

3. Slip the stitch onto your left-hand needle.

Sometimes you have to bite the bullet and unravel your knitting to fix a mistake.

1. Mark the row in which the error occurred, using a loop of yarn, a paperclip or a coil ring marker.

2. Unravel the stitches to within one row of the mark.

3. Position the knitting so the working yarn is on the left side.

4. Insert your needle into the stitch below the first one, inserting from front to back, then gently pull out the stitch.

5. Continue across the row until you pass the mistake.

Reading Knitting Directions

Knitting directions are your road map. Read the directions carefully so you can gather together all the necessary materials before you get started.

Most patterns for garments use "schematics" or line drawings to show the dimensions of each piece of the garment before it's sewn together. These drawings can help you ensure a perfectly fitting garment. (See page 59 in the Win-the-Blue-Ribbon Jacket project for an example of a schematic.)

KNITTING ABBREVIATIONS

Knitting patterns are written using a kind of knitting shorthand. All of the projects in this book follow this format. Here are the common abbreviations and an explanation of the terms and symbols used in the patterns in this book.

beg	begin/beginning	p2tog	purl 2 stitches together
BO	bind off	rem	remain/remaining
CO	cast on	rep	repeat(s)
cont	continue	rev St st	reverse stockinette stitch
dec	decrease/decreases/decreasing	RH	right hand
EOR	every other row	RS	right side
inc	increase	sl	slip
k	knit stitch	sl st	slipstitch
k2tog	knit 2 stitches together	st(s)	stitch(es)
LH	left hand	St st	stockinette stitch
mm	millimeter(s)	tog	together
pat	pattern	WS	wrong side
pm	place marker	yd	yard/yards
p	purl stitch		

*repeat directions between * as many times as there are stitches to accommodate them.

( )When knitting garments, adjustments must be made for different sizes. These will be shown with parenthesis. For instance, the Fun at the Beach Cover-up, which begins on page 88, is sized in small, medium and large. The instructions read: CO 54 (58, 62) sts. Size small is the first number, medium the second and large the third.

HISTORY FLASHBACKS

- The term "knitting" comes from the Anglo-Saxon word "cynttan" or "knittan," which means to tie or knot.

- Ancient Arab traders, knitting as they traveled the caravan routes, carried the craft east across India and far west to Egypt, according to one theory of the spread of knitting.

The Finishing Touch

You're all finished with the knitting, but there's more to do. Careful blocking and joining of pieces when applicable mark the difference between a beautifully hand-knitted professional appearance and that disastrous "homemade" look.

Blocking

Very old blocking boards are nothing more than an 18" x 25" piece of plywood, lightly padded and covered with muslin. You can accomplish the same thing with a piece of plywood and toweling or by spreading a large bath towel on your ironing board.

You'll need a 2-foot square piece of well-used 100 percent cotton sheeting that is pinked around the edges (or even better, an old white cotton feed sack towel or an old cloth diaper), a steam iron and rust-proof pins.

Larger projects will need to be blocked in stages. Any blocking should be done before embellishments are added or before pieces are joined together.

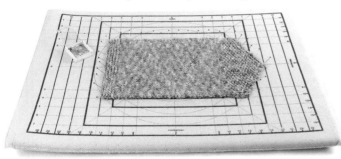

1. Lay out each piece, smooth out to the correct dimensions and carefully pin, placing the pins at 45-degree angles.

2. Wet the cotton cloth thoroughly, lightly wring out and place over the knitting.

3. With your iron on high steam and barely touching the cloth, saturate the knitting with steam. Be sure you never rest the iron on the knitting, as it will flatten out the stitches.

4. Remove the cloth, let the knitting dry thoroughly and then remove the pins.

Joining the Pieces

Seams should be as invisible as possible. Here are two methods that work for most situations.

Method 1 (For Straight Edges)

1. Thread a yarn needle with the same yarn as used in the project.

2. Place the two pieces side-by-side on a flat surface and both right-side up.

3. Draw the sewing yarn through the first stitch at the bottom edge of one piece, then draw through the corresponding stitch of the other piece.

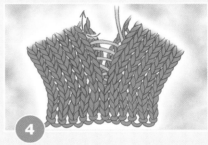

4. Continue to work back and forth, as shown above, being careful not to pull the thread too tightly, as you want some elasticity.

Method 2 (For Shaped Edges)

1. Thread a yarn needle with the same yarn as used in the project.

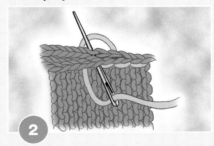

2. With right sides together, use a backstitch, sewing just inside the edge, as shown above. Again, do not pull the thread too tightly.

3. Carefully steam-press the seam open.

TIP

Many of the novelty yarns used in this book are too bulky to use for seaming. Instead, use a matching perle cotton or two strands of embroidery floss.

Embellishments for Pizzazz

Embellishments add the finishing touch to your project and make it uniquely your own. Quite a few of the designs in this book include these added adornments. The array available today at your local craft and bead shops, in addition to Internet suppliers, is astounding. You may already have a stash of beads hidden away or some beautiful buttons snipped off a discarded garment. "If I only had" is a great excuse to browse flea markets and antique shops or shows to find special treasures.

Beads, Buttons and Charms

Beads come in many forms: glass, wood, crystal, semiprecious stones, plastic, polymer clay and ceramic. Beads also come in all shapes and sizes. What they all have in common is a pierced hole, so they can be strung or sewn onto another surface.

Buttons are usually utilitarian, but in this book you'll see them used as pure decoration. Today's button companies have a vast array of designs, from fun to just plain beautiful. Be sure not to overlook the one-of-a-kind charm of antique buttons.

Charms are made of brass or other cast metal and each has a hole or loop, so they can be easily attached.

Use strong cotton or silk thread when applying these baubles and beads. Choose thread colors that are suitable to both the background and the bead. For extra strength, pull the thread through the slits in a plastic beeswax case available at local your fabric or craft store.

TIP
Plastic beads are generally not recommended for use on garments. The wear and tear of everyday use, along with the washing and drying, really makes plastic beads look shabby in a hurry.

Fringe, Tassels and Pompoms

Fringe

Tasseled fringe is an easy-to-make, lovely edge for a scarf or shawl. Once you decide on the number of strands you'd like in each piece of fringe, here's how to put it together.

Finished fringe.

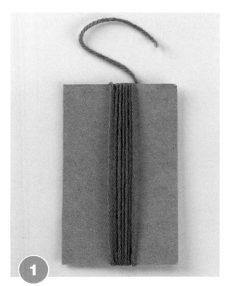

1. Wind sufficient yarn around a stiff cardboard piece that is cut the length desired plus 1".

2. Cut through the yarn at one end and separate the strands into groups needed for each fringe.

3. Fold a group in half and using a large crochet hook (size H or larger), draw the folded end through one stitch in the knitted edge.

4. Draw yarn ends through the loop and pull to tighten.

> **TIP**
>
> You can find many objects around your house that would make a sturdy base for winding yarn for fringe and tassels. A DVD case or CD case are perfect if the size fits your project. A ruler can work for small pompoms.

HISTORY FLASHBACK

Professional knitting in Europe during the Middle Ages was a men's-only club, controlled by the knitting guilds. Apprentices served a six-year apprenticeship, produced a series of masterpieces, and if approved, became master knitters.

Tassels

Much like fringe, tassels add a bit of whimsy to the edges of your knitted pieces.

1. Cut a piece of stiff cardboard the length of your finished tassel and wide enough to comfortably hold one tassel.

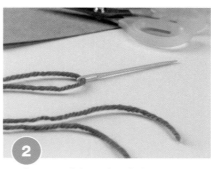

2. Cut a 20" length of the same yarn and thread one end into a large tapestry needle.

3. Lay the yarn across the top of the cardboard and wind another length of yarn around the cardboard to the desired fullness.

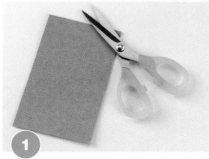

4. Knot the ends of the doubled thread tightly.

5. Cut the bottom edge with a pair of sharp scissors.

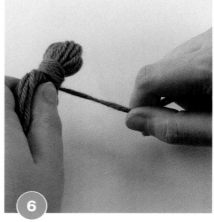

6. To form the neck, wind the end of the double-strand six times around the tassel about ⅜" down from the top.

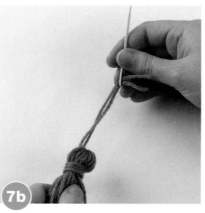

7. Insert the needle underneath the strand (7a) and bring the needle up and out of the center top, pulling tightly (7b).

8. Trim the bottom edge evenly for the finished tassel.

Pompoms

A fun embellishment, pompoms are perfect for hats or in other spots where you might normally use a button. You can make a pompom any size you like.

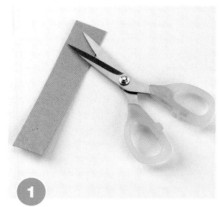

1. Cut out a piece of stiff cardboard half the diameter of the finished pompom.

2. Cut a 12" strand of the pompom yarn and center along the top of the cardboard.

3. Wind the yarn around the cardboard, keeping the tie strand underneath. Stop winding the yarn when it is about as thick as it is wide.

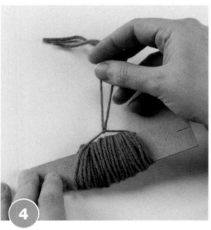

4. Knot the strand tightly over the wound yarn.

5. Cut the bottom edge with a sharp scissors.

6. Fluff the yarn out with your fingers and trim off any stray yarns, creating a smooth shape. Use the tie to attach to your project.

TIPS

- To help keep the yarn strand in place in **STEP 3**, cut slits in each end of the cardboard.

- Keep a record of all your knitting projects in a three-ring binder with plastic sleeves. For each project, include a copy of the directions (write any comments on this sheet), a label from your yarn and a yard or two of the yarn. A picture of the finished piece is an added benefit.

The Importance of Gauge

No two people knit with the same tension. It's very important that you knit to the gauge specified in the pattern, so your finished piece will be the correct size.

Checking the stitch gauge.

Gauge means the number of stitches to 1" and the number of rows to 1". You check your gauge by knitting a practice piece 4" square, using the needles and yarn specified in the directions. It takes a few minutes, but this is a worthwhile investment of your time, as it guarantees you'll have a finished piece to be proud of. Do not bind off.

With a ruler, measure the number of stitches you have to 1". If your stitches match the gauge given, that's terrific! You're ready to start your project.

If your stitches don't match, you'll need to experiment with different sized needles. If you have more stitches than specified, you should use larger needles. If you have fewer stitches to the inch, use smaller needles. Keep changing the needle size until your gauge is exactly right. Once it is, you're ready to start your project.

 TIP Bind off your practice piece and save it in your project binder. Use it to test colorfastness and how the yarn will respond to washing.

How to Use This Book

All of the projects in this book use just two stitches—knit and purl—each by itself or in combinations to make very easy, intricate-looking patterns. The yarns and embellishments make these stylish patterns sing.

Each project contains icons to tell you the level of difficulty, plus the weight of the yarn used. The yarn weight gives you a guide to make substitutions in case a particular yarn isn't available or doesn't suit you. Keep in mind that these are colors and yarns

I chose; you may prefer something else.

Embellishments add an extra fillip to many of these designs. It takes a little extra time, but this is what makes the finished product uniquely yours. Love the felt flower on the purse shown here, but don't want to knit a purse? Add it to a hat instead. These ideas can all be mixed and matched. Embellishments aren't necessary, they're just fun. And that's the whole idea—having fun!

So, pick a pattern, find the perfect yarn and get those needles clicking.

This felt flower embellishment is versatile enough to use on a purse, a hat or even a sweater.

Practice First

Ready to start? Let's knit a fun scarf from start to finish. This is one time we don't suggest a test swatch. With this kind of fun scarf, the gauge isn't important and the scarf itself will be your practice piece.

Materials

1 skein novelty eyelash yarn*

Pair #11 (8mm) needles

8 large gold beads*

Tapestry needle

*Used for this project: Fun Fur Prints by Lion Brand Yarn (color 3650 Citrus) and Darice 1904-21 gold-plated beads.

TIP

If knitting an item as a gift, tuck a "survival kit" in the gift box. Wind a couple yards of the yarn used around a 3" x 5" card and print the care instructions on the card. This way, the lucky recipient will know how to care for the lovingly made gift and will have the necessary yarn if a repair ever needs to be made.

Pattern

- Garter stitch (knit all rows).
- Cast on 14 stitches.
- Knit all rows until 60" long.
- Bind off loosely.

(The abbreviated form would read: CO 14 sts. k all rows until 60" long. BO loosely.)

Add Embellishment

1. Cut the tail 12" long.

2. Thread this tail in the yarn needle.

3. Stitch a running stitch through the bind-off row and gather up tightly.

4. Attach four gold bead with several stitches and knot off.

5. Weave the end at the selvage edge for 2" and cut off the end.

6. Repeat steps 1 through 5 on the other end.

There it is: a finished, embellished scarf. Now you're ready to tackle any of the stylish projects in this book. You knew you could do it!

Hats, Hoods and Scarves

The temperature is plummeting and frost is in the air. It's just the time to wrap up in cuddly hats, hoods and scarves. But instead of using the normal dull and boring colors, try bright and vibrant hues and yarns full of texture, like those used in the projects in this chapter to brighten up those wintry days.

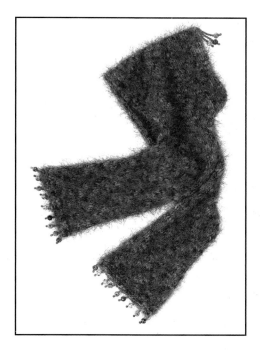

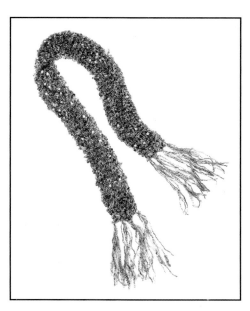

Silk Flower-
Adorned
Hat and Scarf

Sensuous silk
flowers bloom on a
ribbed mohair hat
and matching scarf.
Flowers are oh-so-
easy to make from
silk ribbon with just a
few stitches.

Hat

Finished Size: 20" x 8"
Gauge: 3 sts = 1"

EASY

MEDIUM
4
MOYEN
Medio

Materials

90 yd mohair yarn*

Pair #10½ (6.5mm) needles (or size to obtain gauge)

Yarn needle

1 yd red 2½"-wide silk ribbon

20" green 2½"-wide silk ribbon

Sewing needle

Sewing pins

Matching thread (red and green)

Measuring tape

Scissors

2" x 1" scrap needlepoint canvas, buckram or heavyweight Pellon

*Used for this project: 1 ball Mohair Classic by Berroco (color 1138 Blue, 93 yd).

Pattern

CO 60 sts.
K 6 rows, then beg pat as follows:
- **Row 1:** k4, p2 across row, ending p2
- **Row 2:** p4, k2 across row, ending k2

Rep rows 1 and 2 until the piece measures 7" from beg.

Hat Crown

Beg on a RS row and complete the pat as follows:
- **Row 1:** k4, p2tog across row, ending p2tog
- **Row 2:** k1, p4 across row, ending p 4
- **Row 3:** k2tog, k2, p1 across row, ending p 1
- **Row 4:** k1, p3 across row, ending p 3
- **Row 5:** k2tog, k1, p1 across row, ending p 1
- **Row 6:** k1, p2 across row, ending p 2
- **Row 7:** k2tog, p1 across row, ending p1
- **Row 8:** p2, k1 across row, ending k 1
- **Row 9:** k2tog across row

Cut the yarn free, leaving a 24" tail attached to the knitting.

Thread the tail onto the yarn needle and pull this thread through the loops rem on the needle.

Remove the needle (the stitches are now threaded onto the yarn) and pull tightly to close the top of the hat.

Knot the yarn and begin weaving the two edges together from the crown down to the bottom edge of the hat.

Lightly steam the seam, using a press cloth.

Flower Embellishment

1. Cut the red ribbon in half to create two 18" pieces.
2. Cut the green ribbon for the leaves into four 5" pieces.
3. Cut the stiff material into two 1" squares.

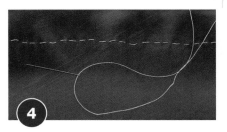

4. Thread the sewing needle with 24" length of the red thread and stitch a simple running stitch the length of the red ribbon ¾" from the edge.

5. Draw up the thread as tightly as possible to gather the ribbon, as shown.
6. Wrap the thread around the stitching several times and knot off.

7. At the knot, pierce through the flower with the needle to the back side.
8. With your fingers, fluff out both the top and bottom parts of the flower into a symmetrical circle.
9. Thread the needle with a 24" length of green thread.

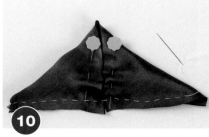

10. Fold the right top corner and the left top corner down to the middle of the bottom edge of one piece of green ribbon, forming a pyramid shape, as shown, and pin in place.
11. Stitch a running stitch ¼" from the bottom edge.

12. Remove pins, pull thread tightly, as shown, and knot off. This forms a leaf.
13. Repeat steps 9 through 12 for a second leaf.

14. Sew the flower to the backing, using several stitches and sewing from the back side of the backing, as shown. Knot off, but do not cut thread.

15. Sew one leaf to the backing from the back edge using several stitches, as shown, knot off and cut thread. Repeat for second leaf.
16. Repeat steps 4 through 15 for a second finished flower.
17. Try on the hat, putting the seam at center back.
18. Place one finished flower in a pleasing spot near the bottom edge and attach with several small stitches, using the thread left on the backing, knot off and cut thread.
19. Attach the second flower to a corner of the scarf about 1" from both edges with several small stitches, knot off and cut thread.

Scarf

Finished Size: 9" x 42"
Gauge: 3 sts = 1"

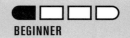

BEGINNER

MEDIUM
4
MOYEN
Medio

Materials

180 yd mohair yarn*

Pair #10½ (6.5mm) needles (or size to obtain gauge)

Yarn needle

*Used for this project: 2 balls Mohair Classic by Berroco (color 1138 Blue, 93 yd).

Pattern

CO 28 sts.

K 6 rows and then beg working pat as follows:

- **Row 1:** k4, p2 across row, ending k4
- **Row 2:** p4, k2 across row, ending p4

Rep rows 1 and 2 until the scarf measures 41" from beg.

K 6 rows.

BO loosely.

Cut the yarn so there is a 12" tail.

Thread the tail onto the yarn needle and knot the yarn.

Bury the tail in the selvedge for 1" and trim off the yarn.

Block the scarf, referring to the blocking instructions on page 25, if needed.

Gypsy Scarf
and Ear Warmers

This duo raises the bar on fun. Colorful, twisty yarns shout, "Look at me!" A multicolored bead fringe tipped with golden coins trims the edges for just a bit more flirty fun.

Scarf

Finished Size: 10" x 42"
Gauge: 3 sts = 1"

Pattern

CO 33 sts.
K every row (garter st) until 42" long or until all yarn is used.
BO loosely.
Cut the yarn, leaving an 8" tail.

Thread tail onto yarn needle and pull it through the last st.
Weave the tail in the selvedge about 1" and trim the end.

Bead Fringe

1. Pour beads into saucer and separate the coins into sizes (the medium size is used for the scarf).
2. Cut a 24" length of thread and strengthen it by drawing through the thread conditioner three times, then pull through your thumb and index finger to set.
3. Knot the thread at the corner on one end of the scarf.
4. String eight beads on the thread, alternating colors, and then thread on a coin, pulling the beads up snugly to the scarf.

5. Go through the coin a second time and thread back up through the beads again.
6. Knot your thread in the edge of the scarf.
7. Weave your thread along the edge of the scarf about 1", make another knot and string eight more beads.
8. Continue across the end edge as in steps 4 through 7 until there are nine dangles.
9. Repeat steps 2 through 8 for the other scarf end.

Materials

250 yd woven yarn*

4mm multicolored glass beads*

Assorted gold-plated coins*

Pair #10 (5.75mm) needles (or size to obtain gauge)

Yarn needle

Beading needle

Sewing thread

Thread conditioner such as beeswax

Small saucer or shallow bowl

*Used for this project: 3 balls Poppy by Tahki-Stacy Charles (color 004 Bright Multi, 81 yd); 6-10697 Czech mix glass beads by the Bead Shoppe; and 1881-20 coins (aluminum coins assorted; gold-plated, 90 pieces) by Darice.

Ear Warmers

Finished Size: 4" x 20"
Gauge: 3 sts = 1"

Pattern

CO 12 sts.
K all rows (garter st) until 20" long.
BO loosely.
Cut the yarn, leaving a 12" tail.
Thread tail onto yarn needle.

Weave ends together and knot yarn.
Finish off by burying yarn in seam about 1" and trim end.

Bead Trim

Embellish the lower edge with bead fringe, using the technique described for the scarf, except use only the small coins and string four beads on the thread, rather than eight. Attach the dangles every ½".

Materials

80 yd woven yarn*

Pair #10 (5.75mm) needles or size to obtain gauge

Yarn needle

Thread conditioner such as beeswax

4mm multicolored glass beads*

Gold coins*

*Used for this project: 1 ball Poppy by Tahki-Stacy Charles (color 004 Bright Multi, 81 yd); 1 container 6-10697 Czech mix by the Bead Shoppe; and 1881-20 coins (aluminum coins assorted; gold-plated, 90 pieces) by Darice.

Jazz, Jazzier and Jazziest Hat Trio

Who would guess that all three of these hats are the same simple pattern? It's just the yarns that are different. So, pick the look that fits your mood.

Jazz Hat

Finished Size: 9" x 20"
Gauge: 2½ sts = 1"

EASY

BULKY
5
BULKY
Abultado

Pattern

Two strands of the eyelash are held together and worked as one. When switching to the chenille yarn, only one strand is used. This is done so the weight of the brim and crown are the same.

CO 50 sts, using two strands of the fun fur held together as one.

Work 10 rows St st
(k 1 row, p 1 row).

Switch to chenille yarn at beg of RS row.

Cont in St st until work measures 5½" from beg.

Dec in the pat as follows:

- **Row 1:** k8, k2tog (k2tog) across row, ending k2tog (45 sts left on needle)
- **Row 2:** p across row
- **Row 3:** k7, k2tog across row, ending k2tog (40 sts left on needle)
- **Row 4:** p across row
- **Row 5:** k6, k2tog across row, ending k2tog (35 sts left on needle)
- **Row 6:** p across row
- **Row 7:** k5, k2tog across row, ending k2tog (30 sts left on needle)
- **Row 8:** p across row
- **Row 9:** k4, k2tog across row, ending k2tog (25 sts left on needle)
- **Row 10:** p across row
- **Row 11:** k3, k2tog across row, ending k2tog (20 sts left on needle)
- **Row 12:** p across row
- **Row 13:** k2, k2tog across row, ending k2tog (15 sts left on needle)
- **Row 14:** p across row
- **Row 15:** k1, k2tog across row, ending k2tog (10 sts left on needle)

Cut yarn with a 24" tail.
Thread tail onto yarn needle.
Thread through the sts left on the needle, remove the needle and pull yarn up tightly.
Knot yarn, weave the seam together, then bury yarn in seam about an inch and trim.

Pompom Embellishment

1. Make pompom, following the directions on page 29. For this hat, the cardboard should be 1" wide for a 2" pompon.

2. Pull the ends through the top of the hat, tie securely and trim the ends.

Materials

75 yd chenille yarn*

50 yd novelty eyelash yarn*

Pair #11 (8mm) 14" needles (or size to obtain gauge)

Yarn needle

Row counter

*Used for this project: 1 ball Chenille Thick & Quick by Lion Brand (color 131 Forest Green, 100 yd) and 2 balls Fun Fur Prints by Lion Brand (color 207 Citrus, 57 yd).

Jazzier Hat

Finished Size: 9" x 20"
Gauge: 2½ sts = 1"

EASY

Pattern

The nub yarn and sequin yarn will be held together and worked as one.
CO 50 sts.
Work in St st (k 1 row, p 1 row) until work measures 7" from beg.

Beg dec, following the dec pat for the Jazz Hat, page 41.
Cont directions for finishing off the hat.

Materials

75 yd nub yarn*

75 yd sequin yarn*

Pair #11 (8mm) 14 needles (or size to obtain gauge)

Yarn needle

Large vintage pin/brooch

*Used for this project: 2 balls Monet by Berroco (color 3368 Beige Tones, 49 yd) and 2 balls Mirror FX by Berroco (color 9001 Gold sequins on white thread, 60 yd).

SUPER FINE
1
SUPER FIN
Super Fino

Mirror FX

MEDIUM
4
MOYEN
Medio

Monet

 TIP

The brim of the hat will naturally roll up, which is just what you want it to do. The roll allows you to control just how much it is rolled up or pulled down on cold days.

Jazziest Hat

Finished Size: 9" x 20"
Gauge: 2½ sts = 1"

EASY

LIGHT
3
LEGER
Ligero

Pattern

CO 50 sts in the blue yarn.

The hat is worked in St st (k 1 row, p 1 row) throughout. Switch yarns at the end of the rows as follows:

- **Rows 1 through 12**: blue yarn
- **Rows 13 through 19**: white yarn
- **Rows 20 through 25**: red yarn
- **Rows 26 through 31**: white yarn
- **Rows 32 through end**: red yarn

Button Embellishment

1. Try on the hat, placing the seam at the center back.
2. Position the three buttons, as shown in the project photo.

When the work measures 7" from the beg, follow the dec pat as used in the Jazz Hat, page 41, but still following the yarn changes. So, you're actually counting two things: the number of rows knitted and the decrease pattern.

Cont directions for finishing off the hat.

3. Sew each button in place with the red perle cotton.

Materials

40 yd red fur yarn*

40 yd white fur yarn*

40 yd blue fur yarn*

Pair #11 (8mm) 14" needles (or size to obtain gauge)

Yarn needle

Row counter

3 star-shaped 1⅞" buttons*

Bright red perle cotton or embroidery floss

Small tapestry needle

*Used for this project: 1 ball each of Zoom by Berroco (color 9199 Bunny 70 yd, color 9257 Kiss 70 yd and color 9230 Blue Note 70 yd) and 3 buttons from JHB International, Inc. (Mega Star 25073 color white, Mega Star 25074 color red and Mega Star 25075 color royal blue).

What Do I Do with Leftover Yarn?

Waste not, want not. It is an axiom proven yet again—this time by three nifty scarves. Use the leftovers from the three hat projects to knit matching scarves. It makes no difference how long the scarves end up. Just follow the pattern from the practice scarf, page 31, and knit to the desired length or when the yarn is gone.

Jazz Scarf

Finished Size: 3" x 60"
Gauge: 5 sts = 1"

BEGINNER

This scarf is the same in size, gauge and pattern as the one shown on page 31, so follow the directions given there. You'll have plenty of yarn. The beads on each end of the scarf are just an extra fillip.

Jazzier Scarf

Finished Size: 4" x 46" including fringe
Gauge: 2 sts = 1"

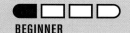
Pattern

The two yarns are worked together as one.
CO 8 sts.
Work in garter st (k every row) until 36" long.
BO loosely.

Fringe Edges

Use the nub yarn by itself for the fringe. Winding the yarn around a CD jewel box provides a nice length. A total of 20 strands results in five fringes for each end.

1. Attach a fringe on the left and right bottom edge and space the other three fringes about ¾" apart, following the directions on page 27.

2. Repeat for the opposite end.

Cut yarn with 12" tail.
Thread tail into yarn needle, pull through the last st on needle and knot.
Bury yarn in selvedge for about 1" and trim.

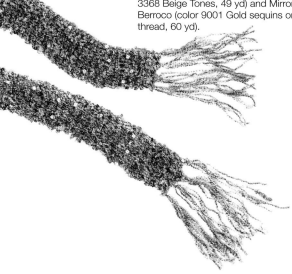

Materials

Leftover nub and sequin yarns from the Jazzier Hat project*

Pair #15 (10mm) 10" needles

Yarn needle

Size J crochet hook

*Used for this project: Monet by Berroco (color 3368 Beige Tones, 49 yd) and Mirror FX by Berroco (color 9001 Gold sequins on white thread, 60 yd).

Jazziest Scarf

Finished Size: 4" x 40" including fringe
Gauge: 2½ sts = 1"

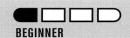
Pattern

CO 15 sts, beg with the red yarn.
Work in garter st (k every row) throughout, following the color pattern:

- **Rows 1 through 10**: red yarn
- **Rows 11 through 20**: white yarn
- **Rows 21 through 30**: blue yarn
- Repeat these 30 rows three times
- **Rows 91 through 100**: red yarn

BO loosely.
Cut yarn to 12".
Finish off, burying yarn in selvedge.

Materials

Leftover fur yarn from the Jazziest Hat project*

Pair #15 (10mm) 10" needles

Yarn needle

Row counter

*Used for this project: 3 colors of Zoom by Berroco (color 9199 Bunny, color 9257 Kiss and color 9230 Blue Note).

Beaded Mobius Scarf

This versatile scarf, which is edged with beads, forms a continuous one-sided surface. It's simply a loop with a half-twist that rests comfortably folded around your head and neck. Named after the German mathematician August Ferdinand Mobius (1790-1868), the shape was first used in knitting by the late Elizabeth Zimmerman.

Beaded Mobius Scarf

Finished Size: 12" x 42"
Gauge: 3¾ sts = 1"

EASY

MEDIUM
4
MOYEN
Medio

Pattern

This scarf is knitted in seed stitch, sometimes called moss stitch, which is detailed on page 19. The pattern shows to slip the first stitch of each row. This results in a neater selvedge.
CO 43 sts.
For every row: sl the first st and then k1, p1 across row, ending p 1 (sts will automatically fall correctly).

Note: To sl the first st, insert the RH needle into the st as if to k. Slide the st from the LH to the RH needle without working.
Work until scarf measures 42".
BO loosely.
Cut yarn with a 30" tail and finish off last st.
Block the scarf carefully, as instructed on page 25.

Materials

330 yd silk/mohair plied yarn*

Pair #9 (5.25mm) 14" needles

Yarn needle

Yarn pins or long sewing pins

Sewing thread to match yarn

Sewing needle

Thread conditioner such as beeswax

175 teardrop glass beads*

*Used for this project: 3 balls Silk Garden by Noro (color 8 blue/green/turquoise, 110 yd) and 3 packages No. 83018 Emerald teardrop glass beads by Bead Heaven.

Join the Scarf

1. Lay the scarf out straight.
2. Turn the bottom edge 180 degrees so the back side is now on top.
3. Join the bottom edge to the top edge with pins. You have put a half twist in the loop formed, which gives the scarf its name for the Mobius curve and its versatility.
4. Thread tail onto yarn needle and weave seam together.

Bead Embellishment

1. Cut a 24" length of sewing thread and run through the beeswax several times to condition.
2. Beginning at the seam, sew a bead to the edge, pulling up snugly and passing through the bead twice.

3. Knot and weave the thread ½" along the edge and attach the next bead.
4. Repeat steps 2 and 3 until back at the beginning.

Detail of the beaded edge.

For more protection from the elements, wrap the mobius scarf around your neck, as shown at left.

Red Riding Hooded Scarf

What could be better than a warm hood and scarf all in one? This is just what you'll need for winter's blustery days. Colorful lampwork beads decorate the scarf ends and tip of the hood.

Red Riding Hooded Scarf

Finished Size: 11" x 33"
Gauge: 2 sts = 1"

INTERMEDIATE

Pattern

Note: Slip the first stitch of each row, as detailed on page 21, for a neater selvedge.
CO 24 sts.
K 6 rows.
Work in St st (k 1 row, p 1 row) until scarf measures 22" from the beg.
CO 8 sts.

Cont in St st for 20" from the 8-st CO. This forms the hood portion of the scarf.
On a RS row, BO the first 8 sts.
Cont in St st for 21" from the BO.
K 6 rows.
BO loosely.
Weave in ends and block, as detailed on page 25.

Join the Scarf

1. Fold the scarf in half, wrong-side out.
2. Pin the back of the hood together from the top edge and across the bottom to the edge of the scarf.

3. With matching perle cotton, stitch the edges together.

Beaded Scarf Dangles

1. Condition a 24" length of thread and attach at corner.
2. String a faceted bead, a 14mm bead and a teardrop bead, pulling snugly against the scarf.
3. Run a second time through the teardrop and go back up through the other two beads.
4. Knot at the scarf.
5. Continue across the edge spacing the dangles evenly.

Detail of the beaded scarf edge.

Beaded Hood Tassel

1. Attach the conditioned thread at the hood peak.
2. String eight faceted beads, the 14mm bead and a teardrop.
3. Run through the teardrop a second time and up through all the beads.
4. Knot at the hood.
5. Repeat steps 2 through 4 for two more strings in the same spot.

Detail of the beading on the tip of the hood.

Materials

200 yd wool blend bulky multicolor yarn*

200 yd eyelash yarn*

Pair #13 (9mm) 14" needles (or size to obtain gauge)

Yarn needle

Yarn pins or sewing pins

Matching perle cotton

21 14mm multicolor glass dot beads*

21 teardrop glass beads

42 6mm faceted glass beads

Beading needle

Sewing thread to match yarn

Thread conditioner

*Used for this project: 3 balls Musique by Crystal Palace Yarns (color 9169 flame, 65 yd); 2 balls Fizz by Crystal Palace Yarns (color 7128 flame, 120 yd); and 14mm beads (54595 Perles de Verre) by Blue Moon Beads.

BULKY	LIGHT
5	**3**
BULKY Abultado	LEGER Ligero

Musique   *Fizz*

Medieval Times Hood

Think of King Arthur and knights of old, but then think of the female version. This lovely head covering spreads across the shoulders and could be worn either over or under your coat. It's a really pretty and different approach to keeping warm.

Medieval Times Hood

Finished Size: 22" x 38"
Gauge: 3 sts = 1"; 4 rows = 1"

EASY

Pattern

CO 60 sts.

K the first 6 rows.

Cont in St st until work measures 16" from beg.

On the RS row, k an inc row.

K4, inc and rep across row, ending with an inc (72 sts on needle).

St st 7 rows, ending with p row.

K3, inc and rep across row, ending with an inc (90 sts on needle).

St st 7 rows, ending with p row.

K6, inc and rep across row, ending with k6 (102 sts on needle).

Cont in St st until work measures 21" from beg.

K 6 rows.

BO loosely.

Finish off yarn.

Block the hood, as detailed on page 25.

Weave back sides together.

Lightly steam the seam, using a pressing cloth.

Materials

300 yd bulky weight wool yarn*

Pair #10 (5.75mm) 14" needles

Row counter

Yarn needle

2 yd length matching tapestry wool

Yarn pins or sewing pins

*Used for this project: 1 skein Thick & Thin by Cherry Tree Hill (color African Gray, 300 yd).

Straight from the Steppes Hat

Nomadic tribesmen thundering across the central Asian plains created the vision that inspired this handsome hat. The brim is rolled and can be stuffed to keep its rounded shape.

Straight from the Steppes Hat

Finished Size: 7" high crown, 21" at the hatband
Gauge: 2 sts = 1"; 3 rows = 1"

EASY

SUPER BULKY
6
SUPER BULKY
Super Abultado

Pattern

CO 56 sts.

Work in rev St st (p 1 row, k 1 row) for 6½". This forms the brim.

Dec for the hatband on a RS row, as follows:

- k6, k2tog across row (49 sts on needle)
- p2tog, p5 across row (42 sts on needle)

Work in St st (k 1 row, p 1 row) for 5", ending with a p row.

Dec for the crown, as follows:

- **Row 1**: k6, k2tog across row (35 sts on needle)
- **Row 2**: p2tog, p5 across row (30 sts on needle)
- **Row 3**: k4, k2tog across row (25 sts on needle)
- **Row 4**: p2tog, p3 across row (20 sts on needle)

- **Row 5**: k2, k2tog across row (15 sts on needle)
- **Row 6**: p2tog, p1 across row (10 sts on needle)
- **Row 7**: k2tog across row (5 sts on needle)

Cut a 12" yarn tail.

Thread tail onto yarn needle.

Thread through sts on needle and pull up tightly.

Knot and finish off yarn.

Block the hat brim, as detailed on page 25.

Weave up the seam, using the tapestry yarn.

Steam lightly.

Roll the brim up and tack in place.

Materials

100 yd bulky wool yarn*

Pair #13 (9mm) needles (or size to obtain gauge)

Yarn needle

Matching tapestry yarn

*Used for this project: 2 skeins Jazz by Cascade Yarns (color 320 Bright Multicolor, 54 yd).

Two Cozy Ear Warmers

Don't want to squash your hair with a hat? Opt for one of these cozy ear warmers instead, each featuring a different design and stylish trims.

Tassel-Trimmed Ear Warmers

Finished Size: 20" x 4"
Gauge: 3½ sts = 1"

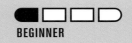

BEGINNER

Pattern

CO 70 sts.
K 4 rows.
Work St st until piece measures
   3½" from beg.
K 4 rows.
BO loosely.
Cut a 12" yarn tail.
Steam lightly.

Beaded Tassel

1. Attach the conditioned thread ½" from the top edge.
2. String assorted beads, ending with a gold bead to the length of 2½". Pull snugly against the knitting.
3. Skip the end gold bead, return the thread up through the string of beads and knot securely at the knitting.

Weave ends together.
Finish off yarn.

Detail of beaded embellishment.

4. Repeat steps 2 and 3 three times, always beginning at the same spot. Additional beads can be sewn down at the top of the tassel, if desired.

Materials

50 yd wool blend bulky yarn*

Pair #10½" (6.5mm) needles (or size to obtain gauge)

Yarn needle

60 assorted 5mm and 6mm glass and metal-plated beads*

Thread conditioner such as beeswax

Beading needle

Sewing thread

*Used for this project: 1 skein Musique by Crystal Palace Yarns (color 9168 Lagoon, 65 yd); 32959-02 filler bead mix hue aqua and 32965-03 two-hole pill bead hue aqua by A Touch of Glass; and 3mm plated beads by Westrim Crafts.

Flower-Bedecked Ear Warmers

Finished Size: 19" x 4½"
Gauge: 3½ sts = 1"

BEGINNER

Pattern

CO 16 sts.
K every row (garter st) until work measures 19" from beg.
BO loosely.
Cut a 12" tail.

Flower Embellishment

1. Use wire cutters to cut the stems off two flowers close to the flower heads.
2. Gently remove the plastic center of the flower, keeping the silk layers together.
3. Push the shank of one of the buttons through the center hole and temporarily hold in place with a toothpick through the shank.

Weave ends together.
Steam lightly.

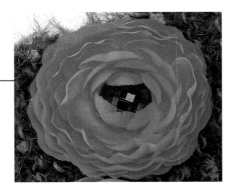

Detail of silk flower embellishment.

4. With the matching sewing thread, sew the flowers securely onto the ear warmer.

Materials

50 yd novelty yarn*

Pair #11 (8mm) 10" needles

1 stem flat silk flowers such as daisy or mum (no roses)

2 colored glass ⅞" buttons with shank*

Small wire cutters

2 toothpicks

Yarn needle

Matching sewing thread

Sewing needle

Conditioned beading thread

*Used for this project: 1 skein Antonia by Skacel Collection yarn (color 3119 Purple, 82 yd) and 45995 buttons by LaMode (color Purple Glass).

Ponchos, Shawls and Jackets

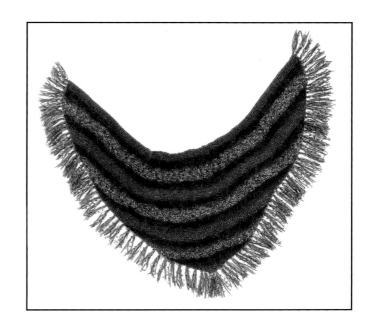

I t's a wonderful feeling to wrap yourself in luxury. Go ahead and indulge yourself, as these pieces are generally easy to knit, but the posh yarns make the garments simply exquisite.

Win-the-Blue-Ribbon Jacket

Silky ribbon and eyelash yarns team together for this jacket, which is sized in small, medium and large. Some seams are tied together with ribbons. Rather sew it all up? Go ahead; the choice is yours.

Win-the-Blue-Ribbon Jacket

Finished Sizes:
Small (32" bust): 38" bust
Medium (36" bust): 42" bust
Large (38" bust): 44" bust
Gauge: 2½ sts = 1"
3 rows = 1"

INTERMEDIATE

Right Front (reverse for left front)

Back

16"

15"

10" (11", 12")

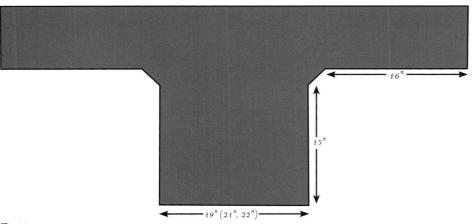

16"

15"

19" (21", 22")

Materials

720 yd ribbon yarn*

720 yd eyelash yarn*

Pair #15 (10mm) flexible needles

Yarn needle

Yarn pins or sewing pins

*Used for this project: 9 balls Deco-Ribbon by Crystal Palace Yarns (color 7237 Jeans, 80 yd) and 6 balls Fizz by Crystal Palace Yarns (color 7224 Jeans, 120 yd).

Deco Ribbon   *Fizz*

Pattern

The two yarns are worked together as one throughout. The sleeves are knitted in with the body. By following the pattern, a garter stitch edge is worked around the front, neck, bottom and sleeves.

Back:
CO 45 (50, 53) sts.
K 6 rows.
Cont in St st until work measures 15" from the beg.

On RS row, inc (k into the front and the back of the same st) at both the first and last st of the k row 6 times, continuing in St st.
On RS, CO 42 (45, 47) sts and k across row for sleeve.
On WS, CO 40 (45, 47) sts and then work sleeve pat as follows:
- **Row 1**: k across row
- **Row 2**: k6, p across row and k last 6 sts
- **Rep rows 1 and 2** until sleeve measures 5¼" from beg

K 6 rows.
BO loosely.
Cut a 12" tail.
Finish off last st.
Weave in selvedge 1" and trim.
Left front:
   CO 25 (28, 30) sts.
   K 6 rows, then begin pat as follows:
- **Row 1**: On RS, k across row
- **Row 2**: On WS, k6, p across row
- **Rep rows 1 and 2** until 15" from beg

Inc for the underarm, as follows:
- On RS, k across row
- Inc 1 st (k into the front and the back of the same st) 6 times
- On WS, k6, p across row
- On RS, CO 42 (45, 47) sts and then work sleeve pat as follows:
- **Row 1**: k across row, k2tog last 2 sts
- **Row 2**: k6, p across row, k last 6 sts
- **Rep rows 1 and 2** until sleeve measures 5¼" from beg

K 6 rows.
BO loosely.
Finish off last st.

Right front:
CO 25 (28, 30) sts.
K 6 rows and then work pat as follows:
- **Row 1**: On RS, k across row
- **Row 2**: On WS, p across row, k last 6 sts
- **Rep rows 1 and 2** until 15" from beg

Inc for the underarm, as follows:
- On RS, inc the first st and k across row 6 times.

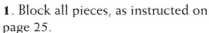

- On WS, p across row, k the last 6 sts

On WS, CO 42 (45, 47) sts and then work sleeve pat as follows:
- **Row 1**: On WS, k6, p across row
- **Row 2**: On RS, k2tog first 2 sts, k across row
- **Rep rows 1 and 2** until sleeve measure 5¼" from beg

K 6 rows.
BO loosely.
Finish off.

TIP

Three sleeves? Remember, you are knitting three pieces: two sleeves on the back, one sleeve on the left front and one sleeve on the right front.

Assembly

1. Block all pieces, as instructed on page 25.
2. Pin the back to each of the front pieces at the tops of the sleeves with wrong sides together.

3. Using ribbon yarn alone, weave the pieces together.
4. Pin the underarms and sides together.
5. Weave each side seam together.

Fringe Embellishment

1. Wind ribbon yarn around a CD jewel case.
2. Create fringe, as instructed on page 27. Each fringe for this jacket has two strands.

3. Attach fringe every ¾", joining the underarm seam.

Colorful Summer Poncho

This short, lightweight poncho is the perfect cover-up for bare summer dressing. It would also work as a beach top. The yarn used is unique: short lengths of blending yarns tied together making a colorful whole. Golden beads trim all of the edges.

Colorful Summer Poncho

Finished Size: 40" x 16" before assembly
Gauge: 2½" = 1"
3 rows = 1"

INTERMEDIATE

LIGHT
3
LEGER
Ligero

Pattern

CO 100 sts on #11 needles.
Switch to #13 needles and p the
    first row.
K all rows thereafter until work
    reaches 16" from the beg.
Bind off loosely.

Cut yarn with a 12" tail.
Finish off last st.
Weave into selvedge for 1" and
    trim.
Block the poncho, as instructed on
    page 25.

Bead Embellishment

1. Cut sewing thread into 24"
length and condition thread.
2. Sew beads around the entire
edge every ½", as in the accompanying photo.

Detail of the beaded edge.

Assembly

1. Fold the poncho in half with
wrong sides together.
2. Weave the top edge together for
2" on the folded side, allowing the
beads to turn to the outside. This
forms the right shoulder.

3. Overlap the two loose ends at
the top edge and weave together,
again making sure the beads are
above the seam. This forms the left
shoulder.

Materials

400 yd novelty yarn*

Pair #11 (8mm) flexible needles

Pair #13 (9mm) flexible needles

125 4mm beads*

Yarn needle

Beading needle

Matching sewing thread

Thread conditioner
    (such as beeswax)

*Used for this project: 1 skein Light Stuff by
Prism Yarn (color Jelly Bean, 400 yd) and
#51625 Perles de Verre by Cousin Corp.

TIP

When using the Prism
Light Stuff yarn, there
will be many loose yarns
where the various yarns
have been tied together.
Since this poncho is
knitted in garter stitch,
both sides are the same.
You decide whether
you want the ties to be
part of the design or not
and choose the right or
wrong side accordingly.
In either case, trim all the
ties to 3" lengths.

*Note the unique look this specialty
yarn gives the finished poncho.*

Snugly Triangular Big Shawl

Three different yarns—a ribbon, a brushed yarn and a "flag" eyelash—are knitted in wide stripes to create this large triangular shawl that is then bordered with a rustling fringe. What a useful addition to your wardrobe.

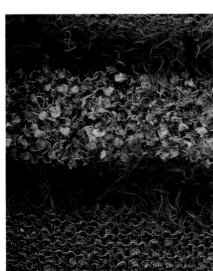

Notice how the differing yarns work together to make three distinct, yet harmonious, textures in the finished piece.

Snugly Triangular Big Shawl

Finished Size: 64" x 36"
Gauge: 3 sts = 1"
4 rows = 1"

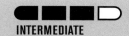
INTERMEDIATE

Pattern

Each of the three different yarns in this shawl—ribbon yarn (A), brushed yarn (B) and "flag" eyelash yarn (C)—are knitted into stripes. The ribbon yarn is used singly, while both the other yarns are worked double (two strands worked as one). Garter stitch is used throughout.
CO 2 sts with (A).
K every row, inc 1 st at both the beg and end of each row (2 inc per row), using the yarn pat as follows:
- k 12 rows (A)
- k 6 rows (B) (2 strands as 1)
- k 10 rows (C) (2 strands as 1)
- k 6 rows (B) (2 strands as 1)

- k 12 rows (A)
- k 6 rows (B)
- k 10 rows (C)
- k 6 rows (B)
- k 12 rows (A)

Inc 1 st at the beg of every row (1 inc per row), using the yarn pat as follows:
- k 6 rows (B)
- k 10 rows (C)
- k 6 rows (B)
- k 12 rows (A)

(At this point, 114 rows have been k and there are 194 sts on the needles.)
BO loosely.
Finish off the last st.
Weave in the end and trim.

Fringe Embellishment

1. Wrap the yarns lengthwise around a DVD box for a finished 7½" fringe.
2. Create fringe, as instructed on page 27. Each fringe is made up of two strands of (A) and one strand of (C).
3. Attach fringe every ¾", beginning at one edge and around three sides. Make sure there is a fringe at both ends and at the point.

Materials

500 yd ribbon yarn (A)*

500 yd brushed yarn (B)*

700 yd "flag" eyelash yarn (C)*

Pair #13 (9mm) flexible needles (or size to obtain gauge)

Row counter

Yarn needle

Size J crochet hook

*Used for this project: 6 balls of Aquarius by Trendsetter Yarns (color 8144 Blue, 96 yd); 10 balls Flora by Trendsetter Yarns (color 504 Blue/green/chartreuse, 70 yd); and 3 balls Voila Print by Trendsetter Yarns (color 10021 Blue/green, 208 yd).

MEDIUM **4** **MOYEN** Medio

FINE **2** **FIN** Fino

LIGHT **3** **LEGER** Ligero

Aquarius *Flora* *Voila Print*

Sumptuous Checkerboard Shawl

Featured on the cover, this is one gorgeous shawl! Vibrant red ribbon and eyelash yarns are knitted together in a checkerboard pattern with shimmering fringe edging the ends.

Sumptuous Checkerboard Shawl

Finished Size: 20" x 74" excluding fringe
Gauge: 12 sts = 4"
16 rows = 4"

EASY

Materials

675 yd ribbon yarn*

575 yd eyelash yarn*

Pair #11 (8mm) 14" needles (or size to obtain gauge)

Row counter

Size J crochet hook

*Used for this project: 9 skeins Tartelette by Knit One Crochet Too (color 260 Pomegranate, 75 yd) and 5 skeins Moulin Rouge by Knit One Crochet Too (color 241 Red, 115 yd).

SUPER FINE
1
SUPER FIN
Super Fino

Moulin Rouge

MEDIUM
4
MOYEN
Medio

Tartelette

Pattern

The shawl is worked in a checkerboard pattern, using the two yarns held together as one.
CO 60 sts.
K 4 rows and then beg pat, as follows:

- **Rows 1 through 8**: k6, p6, rep across row
- **Rows 9 through 16**: p6, k6, rep across row
- **Rep rows 1 through 16**, until shawl measures 36 2" squares (72")

K 4 rows.
BO loosely.

Tasseled Fringe

Yarn groups for the fringe have eight strands of ribbon spaced four stitches apart.
1. Wind ribbon around a piece of heavy cardboard that is cut 8" long.
2. Cut through the yarn at one end and separate into groups of four strands each.

3. Repeat steps 1 and 2 as needed.
4. Use the crochet hook to attach fringe to both ends of the shawl four stitches apart, as instructed on page 27.
5. Trim, if needed.

The shimmer of the fringe comes from the sheen of the ribbon used.

Chill-Chaser Shoulder Shrug

Have you ever noticed how it's just your shoulders that get chilly? This handy shrug fits the bill for those cool summer evenings. The pattern also makes for a comfy bed jacket.

Chill-Chaser Shoulder Shrug

Finished Sizes:
Small (32" bust): 52" from cuff to cuff
Medium (36" bust): 54" from cuff to cuff
Large (38" bust): 56" from cuff to cuff
Gauge: 2½ sts = 1"

INTERMEDIATE

MEDIUM
4
MOYEN
Medio

Pattern

CO 20 sts, using #11 (8mm) needles.

K 8 rows.

Switch to #15 needles and beg St st (k 1 row, p 1 row). Inc 1 st at the beg and end of each k row until there are 50 sts on the needle.

Cont in St st for 20 (22, 24) additional rows.

Place a st marker in the st at the beg and end of the row. This marks the end of the sleeve.

Cont in St st until work measures 19" (20", 21") from marker (ending with a WS row).

Place a st marker in the st at the beg and end of the row. This marks the beg of the second sleeve.

Cont in St st for 20 (22, 24) additional rows.

Beg sleeve dec: k the first 2 and the last 2 sts tog in each k row, continuing in St st until 20 sts rem on the needle.

Switch to #11 needles and k 8 rows.

BO loosely.

Cut a 12" tail.

Finish off last st.

Weave about 1" in selvedge and trim.

Block, as instructed on page 25, to measurements.

Materials

440 yd bulky novelty yarn*

Pair #11 (8mm) 10" needles

Pair #15 (10mm) flexible needles

Row counter

4 stitch markers

Yarn needle

Matching perle cotton thread

Yarn pins or sewing pins

*Used for this project: 10 balls Ice by Cascade Yarns (color 1432 Aqua/Pink, 44 yd).

Assembly

1. Match the stitch markers on each sleeve and pin together.
2. Weave the seams together, using matching thread.
3. Press seam lightly.

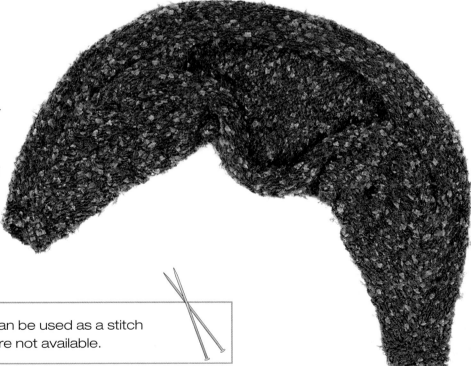

TIP

A contrasting yarn tie can be used as a stitch marker if plastic ones are not available.

Many, Many Colors Triangular Shawl

This small shawl can be tied every which way for great effect. The fabulous yarn is actually made with short lengths of blending color yarns tied together. The tails are trimmed evenly, adding a second look to the reverse side. Golden metal leaves trim the edges.

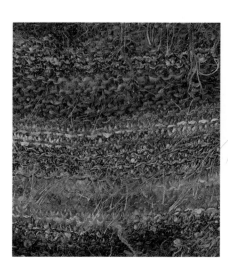

The distinctive yarn works up into an interesting finished look

Many, Many Colors Triangular Shawl

Finished Size: 44" x 24"
Gauge: 2½ sts = 1"

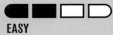

EASY

MEDIUM
4
MOYEN
Medio

Materials

300 yd novelty yarn*

Pair #11 (8mm) flexible needles

120 metal spacer leaves*

Yarn needle

Thread conditioner

Sewing needle

Sewing thread to match

*Used for this project: Wild Stuff by Prism Yarn (color Brass, 300 yd) and G Spacers Leaves Fermeture De Metal by Blue Moon Beads.

Pattern

The shawl is worked in garter stitch (k all rows), making it totally reversible. Since the yarn used has many pieces of yarn tied together, there are many loose ends giving a different look to the reverse side.

CO 1 st.
K all rows, inc 1 st at the beg of each row.
K until size desired or until there is enough yarn left to BO.

BO loosely.
Finish off the last st.
Cut a short tail.
Weave end in selvedge and trim.

Beaded Edge

1. Cut length of thread and condition it.
2. Sew metal leaves to the outside edges every ¾". Do not sew beads on the bound-off edge, as that is the top edge of the shawl.

Detail of the golden metal leaf beads that trim the edges.

Not-So-Basic Black Wrap

Furry black yarn tipped with silvery threads is knitted into a dressy wrap that you'll use for years to come. Tassels embellish the ends for added flair. Worked in easy-to-do garter stitch, this wrap comes together quickly.

Not-So-Basic Black Wrap

Finished Size: 68" x 23½"
Gauge: 3 sts = 1"
4 rows = 1"

EASY

Pattern

CO 1 st.

K in garter st (k all rows), inc 1 st at the beg of each row.

Cont until work measures 24" from the beg and there are 70 sts on the needle.

Work straight (no more inc) for an additional 20".

Beaded Tassel

1. Condition the thread and knot the end into the end of the wrap.

2. String 12 faceted beads on the thread, add a leaf bead and run thread through twice.

3. Snug the beads up to the piece.

4. Run the thread back up through the beads and knot off.

5. String two more dangles at the same spot, following steps 2 through 4.

6. Repeat the entire process to make another tassel on the other end.

Dec sts, as follows:
- k2tog at the beg of each row until 1 st rem

Cut a short tail.

Finish off last st.

Weave end into selvedge and trim.

Materials

500 yd fur yarn*

Pair #15 (10mm) flexible needles

Yarn needle

Thread conditioner

Matching sewing thread

Bead needle

36 faceted 5mm glass beads

3 leaf-shaped glass beads

*Used for this project: 5 balls Moda-Dea Zing by Coats (color 1887 midnight, 98 yd).

Matching tassels on both ends provide just enough added elegance to a piece that's already beautiful by itself.

Punched-Up Poncho

Variegated ribbon and eyelash yarns combine in a medium-weight poncho to toss on whenever a bit of warmth would feel good. Neutral colors make this a go-with-everything addition to your wardrobe.

Punched-Up Poncho

Finished Size: 2 rectangles each 20" x 30"
Gauge: 2½" = 1"

EASY

Pattern

CO 50 sts with 2 strands held
   tog as 1.
K 8 rows.
Beg body pat, as follows:
- **Row 1**: k across row
- **Row 2**: k6, p across row, k last 6 sts
- **Rep rows 1 and 2** pat 57 times.

K 8 rows.
BO loosely.
Cut short tail.
Finish off last st.
Weave end into selvedge and trim.
Follow these same pat instructions
   for second rectangular piece.
Block the two pieces.

Assembly

1. Place stitch markers, as shown on the diagram, 20" from the short edge of the rectangle.
2. Attach A to A, as shown, pin and weave edges together.
3. Join B to B, as shown.
4. Lightly steam seams.

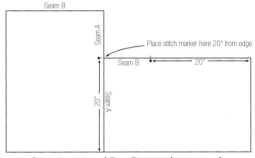

Seam A to A and B to B ... result is a poncho

Materials

630 yd variegated ribbon*

630 yd eyelash yarn*

Pair #15 flexible needles

Row counter

Yarn needle

2 stitch markers

Yarn pins or sewing pins

*Used for this project: 6 balls Zen by Berroco (color 8108 Raku Mix, 110 yd) and 10 balls Plume FX by Berroco (color 6705 Honeysuckle, 63 yd).

Zen

Plume FX

Toasty Toes

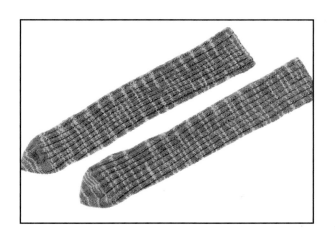

Do you think knitting socks is challenging? If so, tube socks are your answer. They're knitted flat and seamed up the back. Knit one pair, and you'll never stop. Add legwarmers, slipper socks and slippers, and you'll stay toasty all winter long.

Sun, Moon and Stars
Charmed Tube Socks

Golden charms trim these quick-
to-knit socks. They are colorful and
comfortable. What more can you ask?

Sun, Moon and Stars Charmed Tube Socks

Finished Size: 18½" long
Gauge: 5 sts = 1"
6 rows = 1"

LIGHT
3
LEGER
Ligero

Materials

350 yd worsted wool*

Pair #6 (4.25mm) 10" needles

Pair #7 (4.5mm) 10" needles

Row counter

Yarn needle

2 each sun, moon and stars charms*

*Used for this project: 1 skein hand-dyed Weaver's Wool Quarters by Mountain Colors (color Sagebrush, 350 yd) and 1212 sun charm, 1201 moon charm and 1114 star from Fancifuls, Inc.

Pattern

CO 48 sts on #6 (4.25mm) needles.

Work pat in ribbing, as follows:
- **Row 1**: k2, p2 across row
- **Row 2**: p2, k2 across row
- Rep rows 1 and 2 until work measures 7½" from beg

Switch to #7 (4.5mm) needles and work in St st (k 1 row, p 1 row) for 9".

Dec for toe, as follows:
- **Row 1**: k6, k2tog across row (42 sts left on needle)
- **Row 2**: p across row
- **Row 3**: k5, k2tog across row (36 sts left on needle)
- **Row 4**: p across row
- **Row 5**: k4, k2tog across row (30 sts left on needle)
- **Row 6**: p across row

- **Row 7**: k3, k2tog across row (24 sts left on needle)
- **Row 8**: p across row
- **Row 9**: k2, k2tog across row (18 sts left on needle)
- **Row 10**: p across row
- **Row 11**: k1, k2tog across row (12 sts left on needle)
- **Row 12**: p across row
- **Row 13**: k2tog across row (6 sts left on needle)

Cut 30" tail.

Thread tail into yarn needle, thread sts on needle onto yarn, pull up tightly and knot.

Weave sock together and knot.

Weave end about 1" into seam and trim.

Follow these same pat instructions for the second sock.

Simple charms provide a touch of flash to otherwise mundane socks.

Charm Embellishment

1. Position charms, as shown in the photo at right, or in positions of choice.

2. Sew three charms onto each sock using a length of sock yarn and yarn needle.

Bright, Bright, Bright Ribbed Tube Socks

Vivid variegated yarn with a touch of spandex highlights these ribbed-to-the-toe socks.

Bright, Bright, Bright Ribbed Tube Socks

Finished Size: 20" long
Gauge: 5½ sts = 1"
7 rows = 1"

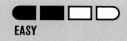

EASY

Pattern

CO 62 sts on #8 (5mm) needles.
Switch to #6 (4.25mm) needles
and begin ribbing pat, as
follows:

- **Row 1**: k2, p2 across row
- **Row 2**: p2, k2 across row
- **Rep rows 1 and 2** until
work measures 17½" from beg

Dec for toe, as follows:

- **Row 1**: k across row
- **Row 2**: p across row
- **Row 3**: k across row
- **Row 4**: p across row
- **Row 5**: k2tog, k across row,
k2tog last 2 sts
- **Row 6**: p across row
- **Row 7**: k8, k2tog across row
(54 sts left on needle)
- **Row 8**: p across row
- **Row 9**: k7, k2tog across row
(48 sts left on needle)
- **Row 10**: p across row
- **Row 11**: k6, k2tog across
row (42 sts left on needle)
- **Row 12**: p across row
- **Row 13**: k5, k2tog across
row (36 sts left on needle)
- **Row 14**: p across row
- **Row 15**: k4, k2tog across
row (30 sts left on needle)

- **Row 16**: p across row
- **Row 17**: k3, k2tog across
row (24 sts left on needle)
- **Row 18**: p across row
- **Row 19**: k2, k2tog across
row (18 sts left on needle)
- **Row 20**: p across row
- **Row 21**: k1, k2tog across
row (12 sts left on needle)
- **Row 22**: p across row
- **Row 23**: k2tog across row
(6 sts left on needle)

Cut 36" tail.
Thread tail yarn through sts left on
needle, pull up tightly and knot.
Weave sock together from toe to
top and knot.
Weave about 1" into seam and
trim.
Follow these same pat instructions
for the second sock.

Materials

370 yd worsted weight yarn*
Pair #8 (5mm) 10" needles
Pair #6 (4.25mm) 10" needles
Row counter
Yarn needle

*Used for this project: 2 balls Fixation by
Cascade yarns (9518 Green/Purple, 186 yd).

Cuddle-Up Slipper
Sox with Sole

Try wearing these comfy suede-soled
slipper socks while you're enjoying the
evening at home.

Cuddle-Up Slipper Sox with Sole

Finished Size: 19" long
Gauge: 5 sts = 1"

EASY

LIGHT
3
LEGER
Ligero

Pattern

CO 47 sts on #8 (5mm) needles. Switch to #7 (4.5mm) needles and begin 3-2 ribbing, as follows:

- **Row 1**: p2, k3 across row, ending p2
- **Row 2**: k2, p3 across row, ending k2
- **Rep rows 1 and 2** until work measures 16" from beg

Dec for toe, as follows:

- **Row 1**: k across row
- **Row 2**: p across row
- **Row 3**: k across row
- **Row 4**: p across row
- **Row 5**: k8, k2tog, k27, k2tog, k8 (45 sts left on needle)
- **Row 6**: p across row
- **Row 7**: k7, k2tog across row (40 sts left on needle)
- **Row 8**: p across row
- **Row 9**: k6, k2tog across row (35 sts left on needle)
- **Row 10**: p across row
- **Row 11**: k5, k2tog across row (30 sts left on needle)
- **Row 12**: p across row
- **Row 13**: k4, k2tog across row (25 sts left on needle)
- **Row 14**: p across row
- **Row 15**: k3, k2tog across row (20 sts left on needle)
- **Row 16**: p across row
- **Row 17**: k2, k2tog across row (15 sts left on needle)
- **Row 18**: p across row
- **Row 19**: k1, k2tog across row (10 sts left on needle)
- **Row 20**: p across row
- **Row 21**: k2tog across row (5 sts left on needle)

Cut tail 36" long.
Thread tail through sts left on needle, pull up tightly and knot.
Weave sock together from toe to top and knot.
Weave about 1" into seam and trim.
Follow these same pat instructions for the second sock.

Materials

275 yd worsted weight wool*

18 star-shaped ¾" pearl buttons*

Pair #8 (5mm) 10" needles

Pair #7 (4.5mm) 10" needles

Yarn needle

Tapestry needle

Matching perle cotton thread

Pair suede two-piece slipper bottoms*

Yarn pins

*Used for this project: 2 skeins 220 Superwash Wool by Cascade Yarns (color 804 light purple, 220 yd); 70555 ocean star beige pearl 3/4" by JHB International; and suede slipper bottoms (size medium, color camel) by Fiber Trends.

Button Embellishment

1. Sew nine buttons near the top of each sock, as shown in the accompanying photo, using the perle cotton and tapestry needle.
2. Attach the slipper bottoms, as shown in the accompanying photo, per the manufacturer's directions using matching sock yarn.

Tiny star buttons embellish the tops of these slipper socks, as you gaze at the stars outside your window.

A suede sole adds durability to the bottom of each sock.

Grab-the-Gold-Ring Legwarmers

Sparkling gold rings add pizzazz to these feel-good legwarmers. Wear them over the knee or scrunched down, whichever you like better.

Grab-the-Gold-Ring Legwarmers

Finished Size: 19" long
Gauge: 4 sts = 1"
5 rows = 1"

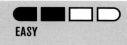

EASY

MEDIUM
4
MOYEN
Medio

Pattern

CO 62 sts on #8 (5mm) needles.
Switch to #7 (4.5mm) needles and work in ribbing pat, as follows:
- **Row 1**: k2, p2 across row
- **Row 2**: p2, k2 across row
- **Rep rows 1 and 2** until 8 rows are complete

Switch to #8 (5mm) needles, start your row count again, set it at zero and begin.

St st in color pat, as follows:
- **Rows 1 through 10**: blue
- **Rows 11 through 18**: gold
- **Row 19** is first dec row. Switch to blue yarn and k2tog, k10 across row, ending k2tog (56 st left on needle).
- **Rows 19 through 22**: blue
- **Rows 23 through 26**: gold
- **Rows 27 through 30**: blue
- **Rows 31 through 38**: gold
- **Rows 39 through 52**: blue
- **Row 52** is second dec row. k3, k2tog, k10 across row, k last 3 st (50 st left on needle).

Set row counter back to zero.
- **Rep rows 11 through 38**.
- **Row 31** is third dec row. k6, k2tog, k10 across row, k last 6 st (46 st left on needle).

Return to blue yarn and cont St st until work measures 17" from the beg.

Switch to #7 (4.5mm) needles and work in k2, p2 ribbing for 8 rows.

BO loosely.
Cut a 36" tail.
Finish off last st.
Weave seam together and knot yarn.
Weave end into seam about 1" and trim.
Follow these same pat instructions for the second legwarmer.

Materials

250 yd worsted wool*
120 yd brushed nylon yarn*
Pair #7 (4.5mm) 14" needles
Pair #8 (5mm) 14" needles
Yarn needle
Row counter
Measuring tape
Yarn pins

*Used for this project: 2 balls The Gourmet Collection Parfait Solids by Knit One Crochet Too (color 1633 Blue, 218 yd) and 2 balls Quest by Berroco (color 9824 Antique Gold, 82 yd).

TIPS

- You will keep track of the rows completed for two reasons:
    1. To make accurate color changes.
    2. To know when to knit decrease rows to shape the leg.

  Be sure to put a row counter on your needle and keep a measuring tape handy.

- When making color changes, twist the two yarns together at the right-hand selvedge on each row, eliminating the need to tie on new yarn at each change. You are actually carrying the yarn not being used up the side.

Summer Gear

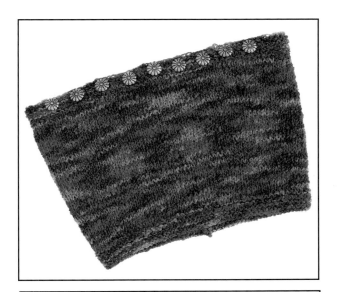

The sun's shining, the surf's up and it's time to enjoy summer wherever you set out your lounge chair. Bright-colored, lighter-weight yarns are perfect for these summertime coolers.

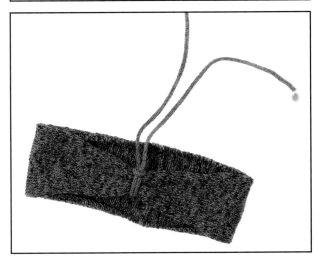

Fun at the Beach Cover-up

Every swimsuit needs a cover-up and this one is a beauty. Brass scallop shell charms are sprinkled over the front. The yarn is a mesh created for summer comfort.

Fun at the Beach Cover-up

Finished Sizes:
Small: 36" x 27"
Medium: 38" x 28"
Large: 41" x 29"
Gauge: 3 sts = 1"
3½ rows = 1"

EASY

BULKY
5
BULKY
Abultado

Pattern

CO 54 (58, 62) sts.
Work pat, as follows:

- **Rows 1 through 10**: k1, p1 across row
- **Row 11**: k1, p1 (rep 4 times), k 38, k1, p1 (rep 4 times)
- **Row 12**: p1, k1 (rep 4 times), p38, p1, k1 (rep 4 times)
- **Rep rows 11 and 12** until work measures 25" (26", 27") from beg.
- **Rep rows 1 through 10**.

BO loosely.
Cut a 10" tail.
Finish off last st.
Weave into selvedge and trim.
Follow these same pat instructions for second matching piece.
Block the pieces, as detailed on page 25.

Materials

725 yd mesh/gauze yarn*

Pair #13 (9mm) flexible needles

21 shell-shaped ¾" brass charms*

Yarn needle

Yarn pins or sewing pins

Matching sewing thread

Sewing needle

Row counter

*Used for this project: 10 balls Summer Net by Crystal Palace Yarns (color 3207 Celery, 74 yd) and 3385 brass charms from Fancifuls, Inc.

Assembly

1. Match two pieces (front and back) with right sides together.
2. Weave a 4" seam at each shoulder, working from the edge to the neck using a 24" length of the knitting yarn. Knot.

3. Begin each side seam 9" down from the shoulder seam and weave until 8" from the bottom edge, leaving slits in each side. Knot.
4. Lightly steam the seams using a press cloth.

Charm Embellishment

1. Evenly space two rows of shells on the seed stitch yoke, as shown in the accompanying photo.
2. Sew charms in place with the sewing thread.

A simple row of shell-motif charms adds just the right feel for a beach piece.

Buttoned-up Tube Top

Silver-toned buttons decorate this strapless tube top that is designed for summer fun—day or night.

Buttoned-Up Tube Top

Finished Sizes:
Small: 28" x 10"
Medium: 32 x 10½"
Large: 34" x 11"
Gauge: 4 sts = 1"

EASY

BULKY
5
BULKY
Abultado

Pattern

CO 112 (128, 136) sts.
K 8 rows.
Beg St st and work until
6½" (7", 7½") from beg.
On RS row, k first 7 (4, 2) sts,
k2tog, k10 across row,
end k7 (4, 2).
St st for 1".
On RS row, k first 4 (5, 3) sts,
k2tog, k10 across row,
end k3 (5, 2).

St st until work measures
8½" (9", 9½") from beg.
K 8 rows.
BO loosely.
Cut a 24" tail.
Finish off last st and leave tail
in place.
Block to measurements.
Pin back seam together and use
the tail to weave the seam.
Press seam lightly.

Button Embellishment

1. Arrange the buttons evenly
across the top band, as shown in
the accompanying photo.
2. Hand-sew each button in place.

The silver-toned buttons make a stylish statement.

Materials

200 yd bulky weight novelty blend*

Pair #8 (5mm) flexible needles

Row counter

Yarn needle

Yarn pins or sewing pins

9 silver-toned ¾" buttons*

Matching sewing thread

Sewing needle

*Used for this project: one hank Ariel Bulky
(color Fall Foliage, 300 yd) by Cherry Tree Hill
and 90627 Cactus Flower ¾" antique silver
buttons by JHB International.

Summertime Crop Top

This versatile top will become a staple of your summer wardrobe. Moss stitch decorates the boat neck and bottom edge.

Summertime Crop Top

Finished Sizes:
Small: 36" x 14"
Medium: 38" x 14-1/2"
Large: 40" x 15"
Gauge: 4 sts = 1"
5 rows = 1"

EASY

LIGHT
3
LEGER
Ligero

Pattern

The 2 yarns are used tog and worked as 1.
CO 73 (77, 81) sts.
The top band is worked in seed st, as follows:

- **Row 1**: k1, p1 across row
- **Row 2**: p2, k2 across row
- **Rep rows 1 and 2** until there are 20 rows.

St st (k 1 row, p 1 row) until work measures 12½" (13," 13½") from beg.

The bottom band is worked in seed st, as follows:

- **Rep rows 1 and 2** until there are 8 rows.

BO loosely.
Finish off last st.
Weave end into selvedge and trim.
Follow these same pat instructions for second matching piece.
Block the pieces to measurements.

Assembly

1. Pin the two matching pieces (front and back) with right sides together.
2. Weave a 4" seam at each shoulder, working from the edge towards the neck using the cotton yarn. Knot.
3. Weave each side seam, beginning at the bottom edge and ending 9" from the shoulder seam. Knot.
4. Steam the seam lightly using a pressing cloth.

Materials

400 (450, 450) yd cotton yarn*

400 (450, 450) yd railroad woven yarn*

Pair #10 (5.75mm) 14" needles (or size to obtain gauge)

Row counter

Yarn needle

Yarn pins or sewing pins

*Used for this project: 3 balls Eros (color 2026 Red/Yellow/Turquoise Multi, 165 yd) by Plymouth Yarn and 3 (4, 4) balls Wildflower DK (color 46 Red, 137 yd) by Plymouth Yarn.

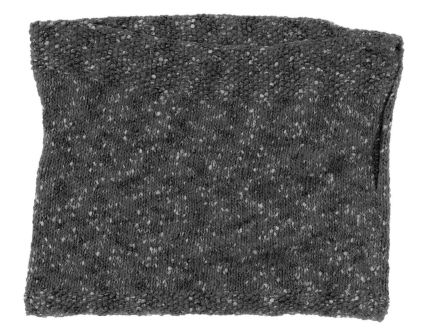

Bare-It-All Bandeau

It's summertime and
the living is easy.
Enjoy this bandeau
for fun in the sun.

Bare-It-All Bandeau

Finished Sizes:
Small: 6" x 29"
Medium: 7" x 33"
Large: 8" x 35"
Gauge: 5 sts = 1"

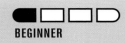
BEGINNER

LIGHT
3
LEGER
Ligero

Pattern

CO 30 sts on #7 (4.5mm) needles.
- **Row 1**: k across row
- **Row 2**: k2, p across row, k last 2 sts
- **Rep rows 1 and 2** until work measures 29" (33", 35") from the beg.

BO loosely.
Cut a 12" tail.
Finish off last st.
Weave the two ends together, weave the end in the seam and trim.

Tie Attachment

1. Sew a glass bead onto each end of the halter tie.
2. Fold the halter tie in half and hold behind the center front of the bandeau with the loop showing.
3. Draw the ends through the loop and pull snugly. This shapes the front and attaches the halter tie.

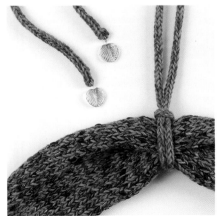

The cord loops around the center of the bandeau and is finished off on the ends with two stylish beads.

The halter tie is a knitted I-cord, as follows:
- CO 3 sts.
- Work as instructed on page 23 until 50" long.

BO loosely.
Finish off last st.
Thread each tail into yarn needle and bury in the center of the cord approx 1".
Trim ends and pull the cord to make the ends disappear.

Materials

125 yd cotton yarn*

100 yd railroad woven yarn*

Pair #7 (4.5mm) 10" needles

Pair #5 (3.75mm) double-pointed needles

Yarn needle

2 leaf-shaped glass beads*

Matching sewing thread

Sewing needle

*Used for this project: 1 ball Wildflower DK (color 101 Turquoise, 137 yd) by Plymouth Yarn; 1 ball Eros (color 3266 Turquoise/Black, 165 yd); and 32966-0 leaf mix glass bead color teal by A Touch of Glass.

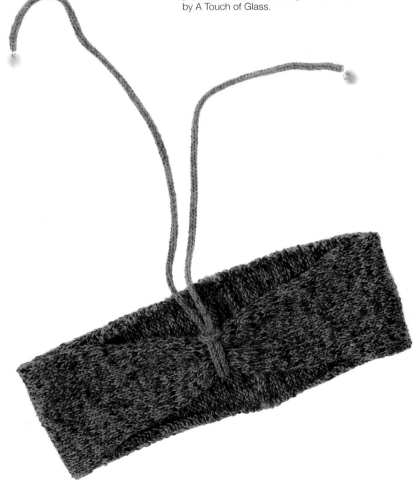

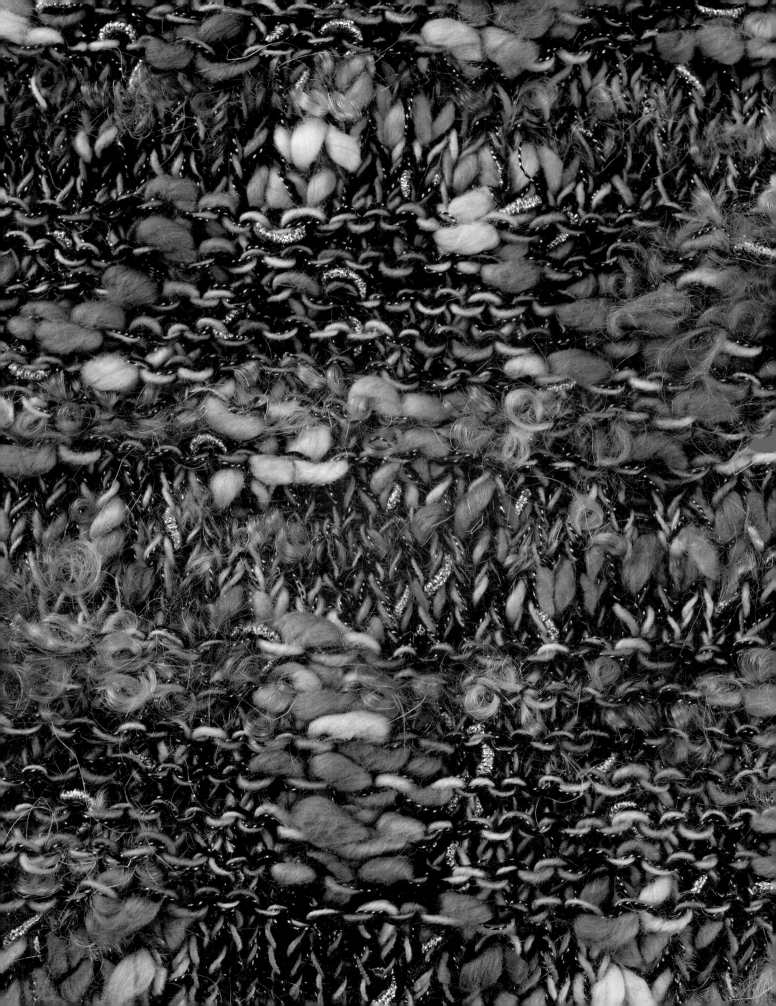

Purses, Jewelry and Other Accessories

F ashion gurus know that accessories make the outfit. A chic purse—or two— is today's must-have fashion accessory. And yes, you can even knit stunning jewelry, belts and headbands to add that boutique look to any wardrobe. The projects in this chapter all are easy and quick to knit.

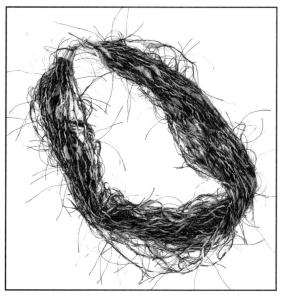

Gypsy Purse

Multicolored beads and golden coins trim this colorful purse. A recycled metal handle provides the finishing touch.

Gypsy Purse

Finished Size: 8½" x 7"
Gauge: 4 sts = 1"

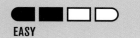
EASY

BULKY 5 BULKY Abultado

Pattern

CO 34 sts.
P first 2 rows.
K rows until work measures 16"
  from the beg.

Flap:
K2tog the first and last 2 sts of
  each row until 2 sts rem on
  the needle.
BO loosely.
Finish off the last st.
Cut short tail.
Weave tail into selvedge and
  trim.
Block purse.

Materials

100 yd woven yarn*

66 multicolored 4mm glass beads*

11 gold-plated medium-sized coins*

28" gold-tone purse chain

Pair #8 (5mm) 10" needles
  (or size to obtain gauge)

Yarn needle

Matching perle cotton

Yarn pins

Beading needle

Sewing thread

Thread conditioner such as
  beeswax

*Used for this project: 2 balls Poppy by
Tahki·Stacy Charles (color 004 Bright Multi, 81
yd); 6-10697 Czech mix glass beads (30 grams)
by The Bead Shoppe; and 1881-20 coins
(aluminum coins assorted gold-plated,
90 pieces) by Darice.

Assembly and Embellishment

1. Turn bottom edge up 6½", pin in place and using perle cotton, weave side edges together.
2. Cut a 24" length of sewing thread and strengthen by drawing through the thread conditioner.
3. Knot the thread at one end of the flap.
4. String six alternating colored beads and one coin on the thread, pulling the beads up snugly.
5. Go through the coin a second time and thread back up through the beads again.

6. Knot thread to the edge for one finished fringe.
7. Repeat steps 3 through 6 evenly spacing 10 more fringe lengths along the flap, making sure one is attached at the point and one at the opposite end.
8. Sew the purse chain on each side at the top of the side seam.

Simple beaded fringe finishes the flap.

TIP

There are four sizes of coins in the Darice bag (small, medium, large and extra-large). The medium size is used in the purse bead fringe.

Hands-Free
Club Bag

This little number is just the thing for the club scene. While small and not at all cumbersome in crowds, it's big enough to hold your driver's license, credit card, mad money and car keys.

Hands-Free Club Bag

Finished Size: 5½" x 4"
Gauge: 4½ sts = 1"

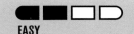 **EASY**

Materials

100 yd mercerized cotton yarn*

100 yd fur yarn*

9 gold-toned 10mm or larger barrel beads*

Pair #8 (5mm) 10" needles

Row counter

Yarn needle

*Used for this project: 2 balls Tweedy Cotton Classic (color 475 Red, 108 yd) by Tahki·Stacy Charles; 2 balls Funny (color 4517 Red, 98 yd) by Swedish Yarn Imports; and 1904-21 gold-plated beads (36 pieces) by Darice.

Pattern

The 2 yarns are held tog and worked as 1.
CO 25 sts.
K1, p1 across row for 4 rows.
Switch to St st (k 1 row, p 1 row) until work measures 11½" from beg.

K1, p1 across row for 4 rows.
BO loosely.
Cut short tail.
Finish off last st.
Weave end in selvedge and trim.
Steam lightly.

 TIP

Always use a press cloth when steaming seams and do not let the iron rest directly on the cloth as you do not want to flatten the work.

Assembly

1. Cut 12 pieces of the cotton yarn 20" long.
2. Knot all 12 pieces together 4" from end.
3. Separate the long end into three groups of four strands each and braid until 8" long.
4. Knot at the end of the braiding and trim second end to 4".
5. Separate the loose ends into four groups of three threads each.
6. Thread a bead onto a group of three threads, snug bead up to the knot and knot below the bead

to hold in place. Repeat for the remaining thread groups on each end of the braided section.
7. Fold the bottom of the purse up 4". Use the cotton yarn to weave side seams together from the bottom edge upwards, leaving a 12" tail.
8. Use the side seam tails to sew the braided handle in place at the top of the side seams.
9. Sew a long bead on the flap front as decoration.

Easy beaded tassels add panache to the ends of the handle on this flirty bag.

Scarf

EASY

What to Do with the Leftover Yarn?

Just as with the hats on page 40, the leftover yarn in this project is perfect for knitting up a cute little matching scarf.

Pattern

CO 8 sts of fur yarn.
Work in pat, as follows:

- **Rows 1 through 12**: k in fur yarn
- **Rows 13 through 20**: k in cotton yarn
- **Rep rows 1 through 20**, alternating yarns, until 84" or desired length

Tassel Embellishment

1. Wind cotton yarn around the small side of a CD jewel case 30 times for each of two tassels.
2. Finish each tassel, as instructed on page 28.
3. Thread the finished tassel ends through a bead and attach one to each end of scarf.

Materials

Pair #11 (8mm) 10" needles
Leftover yarn from club bag
2 large matching beads
Row counter

BO loosely.
Cut a 12" tail.
Finish off last st.
Thread tail in yarn needle, gather the BO end, pull up tightly and knot off.
Weave end in selvedge and trim.
Gather the opposite end in the same manner.

Beaded tassels adorn both ends of the scarf.

TIP

When changing yarns often, carry the unused yarn up the selvedge by looping the new yarn under the old yarn at the end of the row. By doing this, you don't have to cut and tie on new yarn at each change.

Riding the Range Purse

Suede-like yarn adds a western look to this design, which is further highlighted with fringe and silver trim.

Riding the Range Purse

Finished Size: 8" x 6" plus handle
Gauge: 4¾ sts = 1"
6 rows = 1"

EASY

MEDIUM
4
MOYEN
Medio

Pattern

CO 38 sts.
Work in pat, as follows:
- **Rows 1 through 6**: k
- **Rows 7 through 16**: St st (k 1 row, p 1 row)

Rep rows 1 through 16 until work measures approx 18" from the beg, ending with k 6 rows.

Strap:
CO 7 sts.
K every row, sl the first st until strap measures 39" from the beg. (Sl the first st gives a more even edge).
Lightly steam both the body piece and the strap.

Materials

200 yd suede-like yarn*

5 western-style silver-and-turquoise ¾" buttons*

Pair #8 (5mm) 10" needles

Yarn needle

Size J crochet hook

Yarn pins or sewing pins

Row counter

8" x 1½" piece stiff cardboard or foam board

*Used for this project: 2 balls Suede (color 3714 Hopalong Cassidy, 120 yd) by Berroco and 36493 Navajo ¾" buttons (silver and turquoise) by JHB International.

Assembly

1. Fold the bottom edge of the purse up 6".
2. Start with one end of the strap and pin the strap edge to the purse side beginning at the fold.
3. Pin the bottom edge of the strap to 1½" of the purse edge. This forms the bottom of the purse.

4. Pin 6" more of the back side of the purse to the strap. This forms a gusset. The flap remains free.
5. Carry the strap across the top of the purse, making sure not to twist the strap.

6. Repeat step 2 through 5 to form the gusset on the right side of the purse.
7. Using suede yarn in yarn needle, weave seams together.

Fringe Embellishment

1. Wind yarn around a CD jewel case, referring to the instructions on page 27 for assistance, if necessary.
2. Plan for 32 strands of yarn for 16 total fringe sections.
3. Begin at one edge of the flap and attach a fringe every ½".

4. Trim fringe lengths as needed.
5. Space the buttons evenly on the flap and sew in place with the suede yarn.
6. Insert the stiff cardboard into the bottom of the purse so it will keep its shape.

Buttons and fringe trim come together to add interest to the purse flap.

Same Purse Three Ways

Changing the flaps and straps on this simple purse pattern shows you just how easy it is to make a purse distinctly your own.

Purse I

Finished Size: 6¾" x 5"
Gauge: 5 sts = 1"
6 rows = 1"

EASY

MEDIUM 4 MOYEN Medio

Pattern

CO 34 sts on #7 needles.
Work pat, as follows:

- **Row 1**: p across row
- **Row 2**: k1, p1 across row
- **Row 3**: p1, k1 across row
- **Rep rows 2 and 3** for the next 6 rows.

St st (k 1 row, p 1 row) until work measures 12" from the beg.

k2tog at each end of the k row 9 times (16 sts rem on needle).

BO in p st.

Block the purse, as detailed on page 25.

Materials

100 yd ribbon yarn*

Pair #7 (4.5mm) 10" needles

Pair #5 (3.75mm) double-pointed needles

1" gold-toned button*

Yarn needle

Yarn pins or sewing pins

Row counter

*Used for this project: 1 skein Aquarius (color 812 Bronze, 96 yd) by Trendsetter Yarns and 90720 Eldorado 1" buttons (gold-toned) by JHB International.

Strap:
Switch to the double-pointed
   needles.
CO 3 sts.
Make I-cord 30" long.
BO loosely.
Finish off last st.
Bury ends in the center of the cord.

Assembly

1. Turn up bottom edge of purse 5"
   and pin the sides.
2. Weave side seams together
   from the bottom up using
   ribbon yarn.
3. Attach one end of the I-cord
   to each seam.
4. Sew the gold button at the
   center of the bottom edge of
   the flap, as shown.

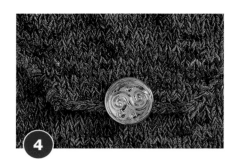

Purse II

Finished Size: 6¾" x 5"
Gauge: 5 sts = 1"
6 rows = 1"

EASY

MEDIUM
4
MOYEN
Medio

Pattern

CO 34 sts.
K 8 rows.
St st (k 1 row, p 1 row) until work
   measures 12" from beg.
Dec for flap, as follows:
- **Row 1**: k2tog, k across row,
  k last 2 sts tog
- **Row 2**: p across row

- **Rep rows 1 and 2** until
2 sts rem on the needle and
k2tog
BO loosely.
Cut short tail.
Finish off last st.
Weave end into the selvedge 1"
   and trim.

Materials

75 yd ribbon yarn*

Pair #7 (4.5mm) 10" needles

54 7mm glass beads*

20 5mm gold beads

Vintage button

Buttonhole thread

Yarn needle

Row counter

*Used for this project: 1 skein Tartelette (color
920 fig, 75 yd) by Knit One Crochet Too and
3 packages 32832-04 glass-striped bead mix
(color turquoise 18 pieces) by a Touch of Glass.

Assembly

1. Turn up bottom edge of purse 5"
and pin the sides.
2. Weave side seams together from
the bottom up using ribbon yarn.
3. Sew the button near the edge of
the point of the flap, as shown.
4. Cut a 42" length of buttonhole
thread and condition.
5. Knot thread securely to the top
of one side seam.
6. String beads on, beginning with
a gold bead, followed by four glass
beads and alternating the gold and
glass beads for a length of 30",
ending with a gold bead.
7. Knot thread securely to the
opposite seam.

Purse III

Finished Size: 6¾" x 5"
Gauge: 5 sts = 1"
6 rows = 1"

MEDIUM
4
MOYEN
Medio

Pattern

CO 34 sts.
K 8 rows.
St st (k 1 row, p 1 row) until work measures 12" from the beg.
Dec for flap, as follows:

- On RS row: k tog the first 2 sts of the row
- On WS row: k tog the last 2 sts of the row

BO loosely.
Cut a short tail.
Finish off the last st.
Weave 1" in the selvedge and trim.

Materials

75 yd ribbon yarn*

Pair #7 (4.5mm) 10" needles

Yarn needle

Row counter

1" red-and-gold button*

30" gold-toned chain

*Used for this project: 1 skein Tartelette (color 667 Denim Blues, 75 yd) by Knit One Crochet Too and 39144 Hong Kong 1" button (color Red and Gold-tone) by JHB International.

Assembly

1. Turn up bottom edge of purse 5" and pin the sides.
2. Weave side seams together from the bottom up using ribbon yarn.
3. Attach one end of the chain to each seam.
4. Sew the button near the edge of the point of the flap, as shown.

Knitted I-Cord Necklace I

This knitted tube can be worn alone or strung with beads or a pendant.

Knitted I-Cord Necklace I

EASY

LIGHT
3
LEGER
Ligero

Pattern

Two threads are held together as one for this necklace.
CO 3 sts.
Work I-cord until 17½" long.
BO loosely.

Cut a short tail.
Finish off last st.
Thread tail onto yarn needle, weave into center of I-cord and trim.

Assembly

The findings kit contains two bell caps, two eye pins and a clasp.

1. About ¼" from one end of the I-cord, wind an eye pin around, put the blunt end through the eye and pull up tightly with the pliers. This holds the end of the cord in a firm grip.

2. Thread the blunt end through the hole in the bell cap and slide the cap down the pin so that the end of the cord is inside the cap.

3. Repeat steps 1 and 2 at the other end of the cord.

4. Slide one end of the clasp onto the eye pin and push down to the bell cap.

5. Grasp the end of the pin with the pliers and form a large circle.

6. Start forming the ring by grasping the end of the pin with the tips of the pliers and roll the pliers down to the cap, forming a ring. If needed, reinsert the pliers into the ring several times when rolling the ring.

7. Slide the clasp into the ring and then flatten the ring with the pliers.

8. Repeat steps 4 through 7 with the other half of the clasp on the other end of the cord.

Materials

25 yd Metallic yarn*

Pair #7 (4.5mm) double-pointed needles

Yarn needle

Ann Norling necklace findings kit*

Round nose pliers

*Used for this project: 1 ball No Smoking (color 106 Bronze, 83 yd) by Filatura Di Crosa, a division of Tahki·Stacy Charles, and Ann Norling findings kit distributed by Crystal Palace Yarns.

TIP

For step 2, you may need to do a little nudging with the end of a knitting needle to make a good fit.

Knitted I-Cord Necklace II

This necklace, which is longer than the previous necklace, uses a furry yarn that gives it added bulk. You can accessorize this piece by adding a vintage pin or silk flower.

Knitted I-Cord Necklace II

Finished Size: 23" long

EASY

LIGHT **3** LEGER Ligero

Pattern

CO 3 sts with 1 strand yarn.
Work I-cord until 22½" long.
BO loosely.
Cut a short tail.

Finish off last st.
Thread tail onto yarn needle, weave into center of I-cord and trim.

Assembly

1. About ¼" from one end of the I-cord, wind an eye pin around, put the blunt end through the eye and pull up tightly with the pliers. This holds the end of the cord in a firm grip.

2. Thread the blunt end through the hole in the bell cap and slide the cap down the pin so that the end of the cord is inside the cap.

3. Repeat steps 1 and 2 at the other end of the cord.

4. Slide one end of the clasp onto the eye pin and push down to the bell cap.

5. Grasp the end of the pin with the pliers and form a large circle.

6. Start forming the ring by grasping the end of the pin with the tips of the pliers and roll the pliers down to the cap, forming a ring. If needed, reinsert the pliers into the ring several times when rolling the ring.

7. Slide the clasp into the ring and then flatten the ring with the pliers.

8. Repeat steps 4 through 7 with the other half of the clasp on the other end of the cord for the finished look shown.

8

Materials

20 yd fur yarn*

Pair #7 (4.5mm) double pointed needles

Yarn needle

2 bell caps

2 eye pins*

Clasp*

Round nose pliers

*Used for this project: 1 ball Moda·Dea Zing (color 1887 Midnight, 98 yd) by Coats; 23113/3 mixed clasps by Westrim Crafts; and 2" silver eye pins by Cousin Corporation.

TIP

For step 2, you may need to do a little nudging with the end of a knitting needle to make a good fit.

Various jewelry findings that are needed when making knitted necklaces.

Gathered Yarn Necklace I

The yarn is the star in this necklace, as you make a positive fashion statement. There is no knitting necessary, so have fun trying another project with yarn and give the needles a temporary rest!

Gathered Yarn Necklace I

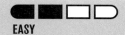

EASY

MEDIUM
4
MOYEN
Medio

Assembly

1. Place the end of the yarn at the top of the ruler with a 2" overhang.
2. Wrap the yarn lengthwise completely around the ruler 20 times, ending back at the top edge.
3. Leave a 2" tail and cut the yarn from the ball.
4. Slip an eye pin under all the threads at the top of the ruler.
5. Thread the blunt end of the eye pin through the eye and pull up tight, using the pliers if necessary. The eye pin is now holding the yarn in a firm grip.

TIP

For step 5, you may need to do a little nudging with the end of a knitting needle to make a good fit.

8

6. Repeat steps 4 and 5 at the other end of the ruler.
7. Carefully slip the necklace off the ruler.
8. Slide one end of the clasp onto the eye pin and push down to the bell cap.

Materials

27 yd novelty yarn*

24" plastic grid ruler

Ann Norling necklace findings kit*

Round nose pliers

*Used for this project: Sorbet (color U1052 Black/Multi, 55 yd) by Trendsetter Yarns and Ann Norling necklace fittings kit distributed by Crystal Palace Yarns.

9. Grasp the end of the pin with the pliers and form a large circle.
10. Start forming the ring by grasping the end of the pin with the tips of the pliers and roll the pliers down to the cap, forming a ring. If needed, reinsert the pliers into the ring several times when rolling the ring.
11. Slide the clasp into the ring and then flatten the ring with the pliers.
12. Repeat steps 8 through 11 with the other half of the clasp on the other end for the finished look shown.

TIP

Any combination of yarns can be used to make these gathered necklaces. Just make sure you have enough total yardage to make the required wraps around the ruler.

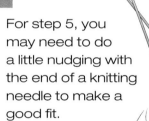

Gathered Yarn Necklace II

A variegated yarn gives this simple necklace a whole new look. Holding the ends and twisting the necklace adds additional texture.

Gathered Yarn Necklace II

Finished Size: 20" long when twisted

EASY

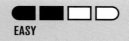

Assembly

1. Place the end of the yarn at the top of the ruler with a 2" overhang.

2. Wrap the yarn lengthwise completely around the ruler 20 times, ending back at the top edge.

3. Leave a 2" tail and cut the yarn from the ball.

4. Slip an eye pin under all the threads at the top of the ruler.

5. Thread the blunt end of the eye pin through the eye and pull up tight, using the pliers if necessary. The eye pin is now holding the yarn in a firm grip.

> **TIP**
> For step 5, you may need to do a little nudging with the end of a knitting needle to make a good fit.

6. Repeat steps 4 and 5 at the other end of the ruler.

7. Carefully slip the necklace off the ruler.

8. Slide one end of the clasp onto the eye pin and push down to the bell cap.

9. Grasp the end of the pin with the pliers and form a large circle.

10. Start forming the ring by grasping the end of the pin with the tips of the pliers and roll the pliers down to the cap, forming a ring. If needed, reinsert the pliers into the ring several times when rolling the ring.

11. Slide the clasp into the ring and then flatten the ring with the pliers.

12. Repeat steps 8 through 11 with the other half of the clasp on the other end.

Materials

34 yd chenille yarn*

24" plastic grid ruler

Ann Norling necklace findings kit*

Round nose pliers

*Used for this project: 1 skein hand-painted rayon chenille yarn (color Sandstone, 181 yd) by Yarns Plus and Ann Norling necklace findings kit distributed by Crystal Palace Yarns.

> **TIP**
> For another look, attach a vintage pin at the center or at one side. With the same yarn, tie a large button at the center. Tie a knot in the middle. Anything goes!

Buckled-Up Belt

A purchased buckle sets off this seed stitch-patterned belt for a trendy look.

Buckled-Up Belt

Finished Size: 34½" x 2" or size to fit
Gauge: 5½ sts = 1" in seed st

EASY

LIGHT
3
LEGER
Ligero

Pattern

Measure waist (or upper hip if this is where you choose to wear the belt). Add 8" to this measurement.
CO 11 sts.
St st (k 1 row, p 1 row) for 10 rows.
K1, p1 across row and cont until the seed st section is the length determined from initial measurement.

BO loosely.
Cut a short tail.
Finish off the last st.
Weave the end in the BO row 1" and trim.
Steam lightly.

Assembly

1. Fold the stockinette area in half towards the back.
2. Insert the buckle prong in the middle of the fold.

3. Stitch the end securely to the back side using the same yarn for the finished look shown.

Materials

100 yd mercerized cotton yarn*

Pair #5 (3.75mm) 10" needles

Purchased buckle*

Yarn needle

*Used for this project: 1 ball Cotton Classic (color 3783 Turquoise by Tahki·Stacy Charles and 341 Western Buckle (antique silver/turquoise, 1-1/4") by JHB International.

3

Fancy Glove Cuffs

Adding these fancy cuffs to purchased wool knit or leather gloves makes them yours alone. Plus, the cuffs keep winter winds from creeping up your coat sleeves

Fancy Glove Cuffs

Finished Size: 2½" x 8"
Gauge: 5½ sts = 1"

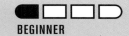
BEGINNER

Pattern

Hold the 2 yarns tog and
    work as 1.
CO 14 sts.
K every row until work measures
    8" from the beg.
BO loosely.
Cut a 12" tail.
Finish off last st.

Use the tail to weave together
    ends.
Fasten off, weave end into the
    seam 1" and trim.
Slide cuff over glove and tack in
    place with sewing thread.
Rep for second cuff.

Materials

50 yd fur yarn*

50 yd woven eyelash yarn*

Pair #6 (4.25mm) 10" needles

Yarn needle

Pair knitted wool or leather gloves
    to fit

Matching sewing thread

Sewing needle

*Used for this project: 1 ball Moda-Dea Zing
(color 1887 Midnight, 98 yd) by Coats and
1 ball Flora (color 1010 Copper, 70 yd) by
Trendsetter Yarns.

*Moda-Dea
Zing*

Flora

Three-for-All Fancy Headbands

Beads and buttons decorate three headbands. These hair decorations are not only easy to knit, but also add fashion flair to girls and women of varying ages.

Headband I

Finished Size: 20" long

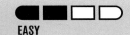

EASY

Pattern

Hold the 2 yarns tog and
work as 1.
CO 18 sts.
St st (k 1 row, p 1 row) until work
measures 20" from beg.
BO loosely.
Cut a 36" tail.

Finish off last st and secure the
yarn.
Steam lightly.
With p side as the RS, fold the
sides to the center and use tail
to weave together, forming a
tube.

Materials

30 yd worsted wool yarn*

30 yd novelty yarn*

Pair #5 (3.75mm) 10" needles

Yarn needle

*Used for this project: 1 ball Zara (color 1401
White, 136 yd) Filatura Di Crosa, a division of
Tahki·Stacy Charles, and 1 ball Bubble Fix (color
8412 Multicolor, 168 yd) by Berroco.

Zara   *Bubble FX*

Headband II

Finished Size: 20" long

EASY

Pattern

CO 8 sts.
K every row, joining in new color
every 4" from beg until piece
measures 20".
BO loosely.

Cut a 12" tail.
Finish off last st.
Join the ends, weave tail into seam
and trim.

Materials

7 yd each of five different yarns*

Pair #8 (5mm) 10" needles

Yarn needle

*Used for this project: 2 cards Adornaments
(color AD40030 Summer) by Knit One
Crochet Too.

MEDIUM
4
MOYEN
Medio

TIP

Each card of Adornaments has 3¼ yards
of five different coordinating yarns.

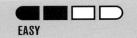

Pattern

CO 3 sts.
Work I-cord until 20" long.
BO loosely.
Cut short tail.

Finish off last st.
Thread tail on yarn needle, bury
   tail in center of cord and trim.
Rep for second cord.

Assembly

3

1. Use sewing thread to join the ends of each cord together.
2. Place the cords next to each other making sure the joins are adjacent.
3. Attach the two cords in three places, as shown, with a button in each spot: middle and 3" to each side.

Materials

50 yd metallic yarn*

3 silver-toned 1" buttons*

Pair #7 (4.5mm)
   double-pointed needles

Yarn needle

Matching sewing thread

Sewing needle

*Used for this project: 1 ball No Smoking
(color 135 Red) by Filatura Di Crosa,
a division of Tahki·Stacy Charles and buttons
by JHB International.

Buy the Handle, Knit the Purse I

An easy-to-make felt flower with button center decorates this charming purse that begins with the purchase of one of many available handles on the market today.

Purse I

BULKY
5
BULKY
Abultado

Pattern

CO 20 sts.
K 4 rows.
CO 1 st at the beg of each row 6 times.
CO 2 sts at the beg of the next 2 rows (30 sts on needle).
CO 4 sts at beg of next 2 rows (38 sts on needle).
K each row until piece measures 11" from the 4 st CO.
BO 4 sts at the beg of the next 2 rows (30 sts left on needle).

BO 2 sts at the beg of the next 2 rows (26 sts left on needle).
K tog the first 2 sts of the next 6 rows (20 sts left on needle).
K 4 rows.
BO loosely.
Cut short tail.
Finish off last st.
Weave end into the selvedge 1" and trim.

Materials

100 yd cotton ragged ribbon yarn*

Pair #11 (8mm) 14" needles

9" x 4" piece red felt

1⅛" button*

D-shaped plastic purse handles*

Yarn needle

Yarn pins

Sewing needle

Matching sewing thread

Awl or hole punch

Scissors or rotary cutter

Tracing paper and pencil

Toothpick

*Used for this project: 2 balls Raggedy (color 9166 Black Jeans Mix, 56 yd) by Crystal Palace Yarns; Art No. 6330 D-shape plastic handles (color Black) by Clover Needlecraft; and 39695 Starshine button (color Black, 1⅛") by JHB International.

Assembly

1. Pin the sides together up to the four-stitch increase in the pattern.
2. Weave together side seams with yarn.
3. Steam seams lightly.
4. Attach handles by folding the top edge of the purse over the bottom edge of the D-shaped handle.
5. Sew handle in place securely with matching thread, as shown.

This simple flower can be made in any color you like.

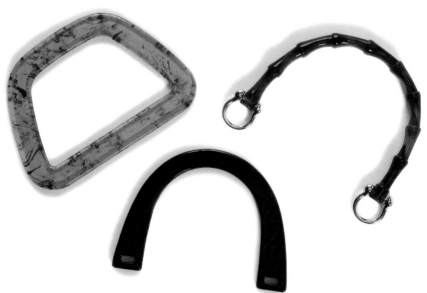

The sizzling trend of making purses has brought forth many wonderful handle choices.

Embellishment

1. Trace the three-piece flower pattern onto the felt.

2. Cut out one piece of each size carefully.

3. Punch a hole in the center of each piece.

4. Stack the three flower pieces with the smallest on top.

5. Push the shank of the button through the holes on all felt layers and temporarily secure with a toothpick.

6. Position felt flower on the front of the purse and sew in place.

Full-size Flower Pattern: From felt, make two of each of the three sizes.

Buy the Handle, Knit the Purse II

There's no such thing as too many purses, especially when they're so easy and quick to knit. This pretty purse is finished in a flash. Just add a store-bought handle.

Purse II

Finished Size: 9" x 8"
Gauge: 4½ sts = 1"
5½ rows = 1"

EASY

SUPER BULKY
6
SUPER BULKY
Super Abultado

Pattern

CO 40 sts.
Work pat, as follows:
- **Row 1 through 8**: K
- **Row 9 through 16**: St st
- **Rep row 1 through 16**
6 more times

K 8 rows.
BO loosely.
Cut a short tail.
Finish off last st.
Weave 1" into selvedge and trim.

Assembly

1. Fold piece in half, matching top and bottom, and pin sides together.
2. Weave the sides together using tapestry yarn.
3. Turn the purse inside-out and stitch across each bottom end to form a triangle. This creates the purse bottom.
4. Center a handle on the top edge of each side and sew in place securely using the combination yarn.

Materials

150 yd combination yarn*

Pair #7 (4.5mm) needles

Bamboo design plastic purse handles*

Matching tapestry yarn

Tapestry needle

Yarn pins or sewing pins

*Used for this project: 2 balls Optik (color 4946 Millefleur, 87 yd) by Berroco and 6327 bamboo plastic handle by Clover Needlecraft.

Resources

Always check with your local knitting, yarn or craft stores for knitting supplies, tools, embellishments and books.

Yarn Companies

Bernat, Patons and Lily Yarns
P.O. Box 40
Listowel, Ontario,
Canada N4W 3H3
www.bernat.com
www.patonsyarns.com
www.lilyyarns.com

Berroco, Inc.
P.O. Box 367
14 Elmdale Road
Uxbridge, MA 01569
www.berroco.com

Caron International
P.O. Box 222
Washington, NC 27889
www.caron.com

Cascade Yarns
1224 Andover Park E
Tukwila, WA 98188
(800) 548-1048
www.cascadeyarns.com

Cherry Tree Hill Yarn
232 Elm St.
Barton, VT 05822
(802) 525-3311
www.cherryyarn.com

Coats Moda-Dea
P.O. Box 12229
Greenville, SC 29612
(800) 648-1479
www.modadea.com

Crystal Palace Yarns
160 23rd St.
Richmond, CA 94804
(510) 237-9988
www.straw.com

Knit One Crochet Too
91 Tandberg Trail
Windham, ME 04062
(207) 892-9625
www.knitonecrochettoo.com

Lion Brand
34 W. 15th St.
New York, NY 10011
(800) 258-9276
www.lionbrand.com

Mountain Colors
P.O. Box 156
Corvallis, MT 59828
(406) 961-1900
www.mountaincolors.com

Noro
Knitting Fever, Inc.
35 Debevoise Ave.
Roosevelt, NY 11575
(516) 546-3600
www.knittingfever.com

Plymouth Yarn
P.O. Box 28
Bristol, PA 19007
(215) 788-0459
www.plymouthyarn.com

Prism Yarn
2595 30th Ave. North
St. Petersburg, FL 33713
www.prismyarn.com

Skacel Collection
P.O. Box 88110
Seattle, WA 98138
(425) 291-9600
www.skacelknitting.com

Tahki-Stacy Charles
70-30 80th St., Building 36
Ridgewood, NY 11384
(800) 338-yarn
www.tahkistacycharles.com

Trendsetter Yarns
16742 Stagg St., #104
Van Nuys, CA 91406
www.trendsetteryarns.com

Yarns Plus
1614 Crossfield Bend
Mississauga, Ontario,
Canada L5G 3P4
(877) 448-4544
www.yarnsplus.com

Embellishments

Artemis/Hanah Silk
5155 Myrtle Ave.
Eureka, CA 95503
(888) 321-4262

Bead Heaven
A division of Halcraft USA, Inc.
New York, NY 10010
www.halcraft.com

Blue Moon Beads
7855 Hayvenhurst Ave.
Van Nuys, CA 91406
www.bluemoonbeads.com

Cousin Corporation
P.O. Box 2939
Largo, FL 33779
(800) 366-2687
www.cousin.com

Darice
13000 Darice Parkway Park 82
Strongsville, OH 44149
(866) 432-7423
www.darice.com

Fancifuls, Inc.
1070 Leonard Road
Marathon, NY 13803
(607) 849-6870
www.fancifulsinc.com

Fiber Trends
P.O. Box 7266
East Wenatchee, WA 98802
www.fibertrends.com

Fire Mountain Gems and Beads
1 Fire Mountain Way
Grants Pass, OR 97526-2373
(800) 423-2319
www.firemountaingems.com

JHB International
1955 S. Quince St.
Denver, CO 80231
(303) 751-8100
www.buttons.com

LaMode Buttons
Blumenthal Lansing Co.
Lansing, IA 52151
www.buttonsplus.com

Rings & Things
P.O. Box 450
214 N. Wall St., Suite 990
Spokane, WA 99210-0450
(509) 624-8565
www.rings-things.com

Rio Grande
7500 Bluewater Road NW
Albuquerque, NM 87121-1962
(800) 545-6566
www.riogrande.com

The Bead Shoppe
Morro Bay, CA
www.CreativeBeginnings.com

Westrim Crafts
7855 Hayvenhurst Ave.
Van Nyes, CA 91406
(800) 727-2727
www.westrimcrafts.com

Knitting Tools

Boye Needle
A product of Wrights
85 South St.
West Warren, MA 01092
www.wrights.com

Brittany Hooks and Needles
(707) 877-1881
www.brittanyneedles.com

Clover Needlecraft, Inc.
13438 Alondra Blvd.
Cerrilos, CA 90703
www.clover-usa.com

Susan Bates
A product of Coats & Clark
P.O. Box 12229
Greenville, SC 29612
(800) 648-1479
www.coatsandclark.com

Other Resources

Craft Yarn Council of America (CYCA)
P.O. Box 9
Gastonia, NC 28053
(704) 824-7838
www.craftyarncouncil.com

KP Books
700 E. State St.
Iola, WI 54990-0001
(888) 457-2873
www.krause.com

The Knitting Guild Association (TKGA)
P.O. Box 3388
Zanesville, OH 43702-3388
(740) 452-4541
www.tkga.com

The National NeedleArts Association (TNNA)
P.O. Box 3388
1100-H Brandywine Blvd.
Zanesville, OH 43702-3388
(740) 455-6773
www.TNNA.org